Lesson Planning in an EFL Class: concorso a cattedra 2020 classi AB24 & AB25

With a Glossary of Educational Linguistics

By this author and available on Amazon.it or Amazon.com:

- ♣ *Five Short Stories*
- ♣ *Blood Brothers Retold*
- ♣ *To Kill a Mockingbird simplified*
- ♣ *An Inspector Calls Retold*
- ♣ *The Great Gatsby Learners' Edition*
- ♣ *Kings, Wars, and Medieval Life: From William I to the Wars of the Roses*
- ♣ *Guided edition for Learners: The Curious Incident of the Dog at Night-Time*
- ♣ *Guided edition for Students: Of Mice and Men*
- ♣ *Of Mice and Men Simplified: with B1 grammar practice*
- ♣ *A View from the Bridge. A Short Story*

Lesson Planning in an EFL Class: concorso a cattedra 2020 classi AB24 & AB25

With a Glossary of Educational Linguistics

Angela T. Wesker

Ω
Independently published
2020

Copyright © 2020 by Angela T. Wesker

All rights reserved.

No part of this book may be reproduced, stored in a retrieval system, or transmitted in any form or by any means, electronic, mechanical, photocopying, recording or otherwise, without the written permission of the publisher.

Every effort has been made to acknowledge correctly and contact the source and/or copyright holder of material used in this book. The publishers apologize for any unintentional errors or omissions and will be pleased to make corrections in future editions.

First Printing: 2020

ISBN 9798606187041

Ω Independently published

Contents

Introduction 1

Key concepts and ideas for planning... 2

A general model 7

A lesson plan for history, the American War of Independence 8

A lesson plan for history, the Second World War and Winston Churchill 10

A lesson plan for vocabulary & grammar, sports and modal verbs   23

A lesson plan for vocabulary, the human body and health 26

A lesson plan for grammar, the passive voice......................... 29

A lesson plan for literature, Hamlet's monologue 33

A lesson plan for a literary and historical period, the Puritan Age 39

How to analyse an ESP text 51

A lesson plan for ESP, economics... 58

A lesson plan for ESP, tourism 64

A lesson plan for cross-curricular learning 69

Glossary of Educational Linguistics 81

References 111

Introduction

Lesson planning is part of any teacher's job. It is important to know how to design a scheme of work for a particular group of students, in which a series of lessons are linked to form a complete programme.

The aim of this book is to help you write effective, tailor-made lesson plans. Indeed, it will focus on how you can get ready for planning and how you can assess your teaching for more effective learning.

The book will provide different sets of lesson plan formats and several practical samples covering different areas of ESL teaching, e.g. grammar, vocabulary, literature, history, ESP. These are only examples to help you plan your lessons. They are not one-size-fits-all resources because planning, and consequently teaching goes hand in hand with the learners' needs.

Key concepts and ideas for planning

A lesson is an organized set of activities designed to present one piece of your course while working toward achieving one or more learning objectives. A lesson must not be confused with a lecture, which is a teaching technique that you can use to facilitate your lesson.

Planning a lesson has a lot of important functions:
1. It helps you organize what you expect the students to be able to do or know by the end of the lesson according to the time you have available.
2. It helps you keep on target, although you can respond to the needs of the moment, if necessary.
3. It is a way of recording what a class has done and what needs to be enhanced. It also helps you with feedback.

You can download your lesson plans from the internet or find them ready-made on teachers' books, but none of them will meet your students' specific, unique, individual and authentic learning needs. This is why it is essential to know how to plan lessons.

When we plan an EFL lesson we need to focus on a series of key elements.

Target class/level
You have been assigned a specific course, or group, or level. Your students and their learning needs need to be always on your mind. Besides, you need to know what they are carrying with them and where they need to go, i.e. prerequisites and aims.

Prerequisites

The word prerequisite is partly based on the Latin verb *requirere*. It means "to need or require". A prerequisite represents anything that must be accomplished or acquired before something else can be done. (from the Merriam Webster Dictionary). It is important you get to know your students. Students are never a tabula rasa, a blank slate even though their level is zero or pre-A1. Your students' previous knowledge is where their leaning path should start.

Each student learns differently. Some need to see the written information, some need to hear it, and others need to get their hands on it. As a consequence, if you want to be effective, you need to investigate your students' learning styles (visual, auditory, tactile or a combination). Some students will benefit more from working individually while others will thrive in pair work or groups. This will help you format activities to different interaction preferences.

Your plan will fit the overall class, but bear in mind you might have to make modifications to account for students with disabilities, those who are struggling or unmotivated, and those who are gifted. Use strategies of differentiation whenever possible.

Aims

Aims are the targets of one lesson or unit of work. Your educational aims include the knowledge, the skills and the competencies that students should have at the end of their learning path. Among the main functions of the Common European Framework of Reference are "to provide a metalanguage for discussing the complexity of language proficiency and for reflecting on and communicating decisions on learning aims and outcomes that are coherent and transparent, and to provide inspiration for curriculum development and teacher education." Use the new illustrative descriptor scale as presented in the CEFR Companion Volume –that includes areas such as mediation, plurilingual/pluricultural competence, and sign language- to list and present your objectives. On the contrary, goals are the targets that learners and teachers have in language learning. These may be short- and long-term.

Timing
Timing a lesson correctly is imperative. To get the timing right, it is necessary to adapt your teaching style to the individual student, as well as to the material being taught. Set your timing in advance, trying to be realistic and flexible –add extra 10 minutes for any unplanned inconvenience.

Methodology
The methodology is a system of practices and procedures that a teacher uses to teach. It will be based on beliefs about the nature of language, and how it is learnt (known as 'Approach').

<u>Activate the given[1] or Review & anticipatory set[2]</u>.
As a first step in your lesson stimulate recall of prior learning and stir the students' interest to create the urge to learn and to gain their attention. This will help students to relax, to set their brain in motion, i.e. to think and to get to know each other. It will also break down social barriers (that may prevent active learning) and keep your students energized and motivated.

<u>Add the new[3] or Input and modelling[4]</u>.

---

[1] Martin Dodman, notes from his methodology courses at the University of Pavia
[2] From Madeline Hunter's Seven Step Lesson Plan and Gagne's Nine Events of Instruction
[3] Martin Dodman, notes from his methodology courses at the University of Pavia

This step is the very core of your lesson. Teachers should select and develop the appropriate teaching and learning resources, providing students with learning guidance. Teachers should use materials to show students examples of what is expected to be the end product of their work. Analysis, synthesis, and reflection are all part of this step to build effective learning.

<u>Assimilate the new to the given[5] or Elicit performance (practice) and provide feedback[6]</u>.

Students need time to put it into action what they have just learnt. Devise activities the students can perform under your supervision to ensure that they are able to practise the materials. If the students make mistakes you can show them how to do correctly. Close monitoring and direction of the students are necessary as they practise the whole task for the first time independently. You may also plan different activities to meet the students' (special) needs.

This is also the time you observe your students working to collect detailed information that can be used to improve instruction and student learning. You can assess the learning process in order to modify your entire procedure to improve student attainment. This is called continuous assessment.

<u>Accommodate the given[7] to the new or Enhance retention and transfer[8]</u>.

---

[4] From Madeline Hunter's Seven Step Lesson Plan and Gagne's Nine Events of Instruction

[5] Martin Dodman, notes from his methodology courses at the University of Pavia

[6] From Madeline Hunter's Seven Step Lesson Plan and Gagne's Nine Events of Instruction

[7] Martin Dodman, notes from his methodology courses at the University of Pavia

After students appear to understand the new material they are allowed to further apply or practise using the new information. This may occur in class or as homework, but there should be a short time between instruction and practice and feedback. This independent production makes the student responsible for their final learning outcomes. Activities can be rewriting notes, completing project assignments through peer interaction or group work. This is the student's authentic learning and he can finally say "I can do it".

At the end of your lesson (or unit, course, program, or even school year), to evaluate the students' learning, the skills they have acquired and their achievement in general, use summative assessments with score or grades.

---

[8] From Madeline Hunter's Seven Step Lesson Plan and Gagne's Nine Events of Instruction

A general model

School name	Teacher	Date	Subject/year/level
Syllabus link:		Lesson title:	
Context, recap and link with previous learning:			
Materials:			
<u>Differentiated Learning Outcomes</u> (specifically targeting the needs of various groups) e.g. linked to grades • Everyone will be able to… • Most students will be able to… • Some students will be able…			
<u>Student activities</u> Outline below what different groups of students will be doing/learning in the lesson to enable all of them to achieve the LOs. Please also indicate how other supporting adults will be deployed to impact on progress.			Method used to assess the students' progress- what is happening in the lesson
Timing	**Task** Starter Introduction to lesson Task 1 Recap		Starter Introduction Recap
Opportunities to develop cross-curricular literacy (e.g. reading, writing, verbal)			
Homework			Due:

Lesson Planning in an EFL Class - Concorso a cattedra 2020

A lesson plan for history, the American War of Independence

School name	Teacher	Date	Subject/year/level History/4th/B2

Syllabus link: the American War of Independence	Lesson title: What happened in the American War of Independence?

Context, recap and link with previous learning: Students have read and completed worksheets on the American War of Independence during the last lesson. They handed in their work which will be handed back already corrected.

Materials: Worksheets and questions- causes, battles, aftermaths &facts. Map as history Site, *The Thirteen Colonies & the United States*

Differentiated Learning Outcomes (specifically targeting the needs of various groups) e.g. linked to grades
• Everyone will be able to **explain** that there was the American War of Independence
• Most students will be able to **explain** the causes of the American War of Independence
• Some students will be able to **suggest** the consequences of the American War of Independence

Student activities Outline below what different groups of students will be doing/learning in the lesson to enable all of them to achieve the LOs. Please also indicate how other supporting adults will be deployed to impact on progress.	Method used to assess the students' progress- what is happening in the lesson
Timing **Task**	
13.05 Introduction to lesson —T discusses lesson LOs (organize make up tests)	Teacher hands back work sheets
13.10 Main Task —1st listening -Teacher	Introduction

	asks students to watch video and create titles for the war	
13.12	Students watch map work	Focus on Map video
13.18	Individual work - Students write down 3 titles	Individual work — T circulates
13.20	Task: Brainstorm titles on Board — Several Students write their ideas on board	Main Task-Board work
13.25	Main Task — Students watch the video for second time Answer questions for second viewing in pairs	Second viewing of Map video & T writes question on board
13.30	Whole Class discuss answers	
13.35	Main Task — discuss questions: what happened at the end of the American War of Independence? Write 2 ideas with the people next to you.	
13.40	Whole class discussion of ideas. Copy ideas from board	Plenary
13.45	Whole Class. T introduces some of the aspects of the aftermaths of the war	

Opportunities to develop cross-curricular literacy (e.g. reading, writing, verbal)
The differentiated activities allow students to work on reading and sorting information

Homework	Due:

A lesson plan for history, the Second World War and Winston Churchill

Prerequisites:
Linguistic (level of English): B2
(with reference to "A Common European Framework of reference. Companion Volume with New Descriptors").

Cognitive: general background knowledge of the historical context in the first half of the XX century. Familiarity with certain tasks (fill-in-the-gaps exercises, matching exercises, double choice exercises etc.) and expositive and narrative texts.

Aims:
<u>Improvement of communicative linguistic activities.</u> Productive: oral and written production (speaking and writing); receptive: aural and visual reception (listening and reading): interactive: oral interaction.

Acquisition of information about the <u>historical and social</u> context during the II World War: the principal events and the main characters.

Development of <u>critical capacities</u> to connect historical events of the past with the present society. through expansion and research works.

Give students useful material and occasions for a reflection, in particular as a preparation for the "Esame di Stato".

Target School: liceo linguistico

Angela T. Wesker

Target Class: V year

Time of realisation: 7 hours

Teacher aids: the interactive white board

The Second World War

First Phase

The beginning of the war was extremely quick and the allies seemed near to being overwhelmed. German forces attacked Denmark and Norway, then subjugated Holland, Belgium, and Luxembourg and struck deep into France, where they turned the French defensive position of the Maginot Line. The British troops who had gone forward into Belgium were obliged to retire to Dunkirk (May 1940), where they were able to evacuate to Britain only with great difficulty. In June 1940 the Germans occupied Paris.

During the days of intensive bombardment, many Londoners sought safety at night in the underground stations.

Ruins in the centre of London following the German blitzes in 1940

Now Hitler planned the invasion of Great Britain. In Winston Churchill, who had become Prime Minister in a coalition government (1940-45), the country found a leader who personified its stubborn will to meet that challenge with courage and vigour. To protect the ferrying of large troops, the Germans needed to win air supremacy over the Channel and southern England and this led to the Air Battle of Britain, which raged in the late summer of 1940 and was a decisive event in the course of the war. Day after day the German attacks were met and turned back by the English Spitfire and Hurricane squadrons, till the Germans lost the initiative and Hitler was obliged to postpone his invasion plans and later abandon them. One of the reasons why German bombing did not defeat Britain was that the English had already developed radar, then unknown to the Germans.

RAF pilot scrambles to his fighter-bomber in Normandy

British football team with gas masks in 1916

On the eastern front, in June 1941, Hitler undertook the invasion of Russia, the so-called "Operation Barbarossa". Early German successes were spectacular, but the decisive battle was fought at *Stalingrad,* where in November 1942 the Russians forced a German army to surrender.

The conflict, however, was not confined to Europe. In North Africa, the Afrika Corps of General *Rommel* had come to the assistance of the Italians. In the *desert war,* the Germans came near to success but in October 1942 in the Battle of *El Alamein* they were defeated by a British offensive, directed by Generals *Alexander* and *Montgomery.* In November an Anglo-American force under the command of the American General *Eisenhower* landed in Morocco and Algeria and in May 1943 all the North African coast was cleared by the Allies. From Tunisia. in July 1943. the Allies invaded *Sicily.* Other allied forces landed at Salerno and Anzio and began to fight their way northwards.

In the Pacific the Japanese had launched a surprise attack on the American naval base of *Pearl Harbor* (December 1941) destroying a large part of the American Pacific Fleet; other attacks brought the Philippines. Indo-China and other territories in the East under Japanese control.

Food rationing

But the Americas were able to gain the upper hand again by winning the two important naval battle of *Midway* and *Coral Sea.*

The Second Phase

By the summer of 1943, therefore, the expansion of the Axis powers had been checked; now the time had come for the re-conquest of Europe, wherein the occupied countries, resistance movements waited for the Allies. The American President Roosevelt and Stalin convinced Churchill that the main attack should be delivered from Britain against the coast of *Normandy.* This enormous operation was again under the command of General Eisenhower, and on June 6th 1944 ("D Day") the landing on the coasts of Normandy took place successfully. The German defences were under the command of Rommel, who had been recalled from Africa, but they were defeated. Paris was liberated and at the beginning of 1945 the Rhine was crossed, while the Russians were driving into eastern Germany.

The Allies met on the Elbe in April. Hitler committed suicide in Berlin and in May the Germans surrendered unconditionally and the war in Europe ended.
There remained the other enemy, Japan. It seemed inevitable that the struggle would be long and then, on August 6th, 1945, the first atomic bomb was dropped on *Hiroshima;* three days later a second bomb was dropped on *Nagasaki.* On August 10th the Japanese surrendered. Thus the war ended and the world stepped forward into a new age, dominated by the frightful clouds of an atomic explosion.

Propaganda posters

Pre-reading activities (warm-up)

Look at the above photographs, say what they suggest you and discuss them.

Wh-questions: What do you know about the II World War? When did it take place? Who won it? Why did it break out?

Scanning activity. Pick out all the words in the text written in *italics:* why are they written in this way? What do they refer to?

Reading activities
Read the text carefully. Then answer the following questions:
1. What was the beginning of the war like?
2. What was the importance of the Battle of Britain?

3. What do you know about the Battle of Stalingrad?
4. What were the main events of the conflict in Africa?
5. When and after what event did the USA join the war?
6. What do you know about the landing of the Allies in Normandy?
7. How did the war end in Europe?
8. What compelled Japan to surrender?

Complete the map pointing out where and what happened during the II WW.

Complete the timeline pointing out in chronological order the main events of the II WW.

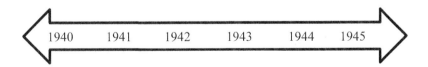

Post-reading activities
Express your opinion

The picture of Europe during the II World War is that of a series of separate nations struggling to get the supremacy one over the other.
Nowadays the situation has completely changed: the European countries have not only put an end to all their divisions, but they have begun a process of economic and political integration, which has brought to the creation of the EU and the introduction of a common currency.

Are you in favour or Euro-sceptical? Express your opinion, even looking for further information about this topic. (You may use the Internet, newspapers or books).

Winston Churchill

"Their Finest Hour"

Winston Churchill is one of the key figures of the twentieth century. Although the United States, the Soviet Union, and other allies undoubtedly played a pivotal role in achieving victory, the British Prime Minister was the first leader who stood up to Hitler and the Nazis. His radio broadcasts inspired a nation and many of his phrases, such as "We shall fight on the beaches" and "This was their finest hour" are as quotable as Shakespeare.

Churchill replaced Neville Chamberlain as Prime Minister in 1940. Churchill was 65 at the time and, had he retired from politics before then, his career would be remembered as an interesting failure. He was born the son of Lord Randolph Churchill, a Conservative politician (as well as the son of the Duke of Marlborough), and an American heiress, Jennie Jerome. After an undistinguished school career at Harrow (the rival of Eton). he entered Sandhurst, the prestigious military academy. He graduated in 1895 and served in the army in India and in Sudan. It was, however, as a military correspondent in the Boer War that he first gained national attention, after being taken prisoner and escaping from his captors. He returned to Britain a hero and was elected a Conservative MP in 1900. He was, however, to "cross the floor" and join the Liberal Party a few years later. He became Home Secretary and, in 1911, was involved in the first controversial episode of his career when he allegedly ordered the troops to open fire on striking miners in the Welsh village of Tonypandy. When the First World War broke out in 1914, he became First Lord of the Admiralty and this led to another controversial episode. Churchill was responsible for the disastrous sea attack on Turkish forces at Gallipoli in 1915. He lost his job and so earned the perpetual animosity of the Australians, disproportionate numbers of whom were used as "cannon fodder" in the attack.

Churchill even lost his seat in Parliament in 1922 but, after switching back to the Conservative, became a Cabinet Minister once again, serving as

Chancellor of the Exchequer in Stanley Baldwin's administration.

The Wilderness
Churchill left office in 1929 and this was followed by what he called the "wilderness years". When Hitler came to power in Germany in 1933, he was one of a minority of people who understood the Nazi menace, but his warnings fell on deaf ears. The British followed a policy of "appeasement" but, once Hitler's intentions became clear, they realised that Churchill was the man to lead them. Victory over Hitler was achieved in 1945, but the British were to prove ungrateful, A general election was held and, much to his horror, the 71-year-old leader was defeated by a landslide. Never one to give up, he returned to Downing Street in 1951 and resigned for reasons of health in 1954. When he died 11 years later, he was given a full state funeral. He was the first "commoner" to receive such an honour since the Duke of Wellington, the man who defeated Napoleon at Waterloo.

Prime Minister Winston Churchill, President Franklin D. Roosevelt and Marshal Josef Stalin left to the right — as they appeared at the Yalta Conference in the Crimea., on the Black sea coast, where they met in February 1945 to plan the final defeat of Nazi Germany and discuss the general political establishment for the post war years.

Pre-reading activities

Try to give an answer to the following question. What do you know about Winston Churchill?

Vocabulary activity. Read the text very quickly and underline the words you don't know. Guess their meaning. Below you may find a list of the words you probably don't know, match them with the most suitable definition.

1. Pivotal
2. Radio broadcasts
3. Quotable
4. Heiress
5. Failure
6. Home Secretary
7. Allegedly
8. Striking miners
9. Cannon fodder
10. Exchequer
11. Wilderness Year
12. Appeasement
13. By a landslide
14. Commoner

a. Very rich woman
b. Without noble origins
c. Years spent without any public involvement
d. Essential
e. Programme on the radio
f. Winning a political election with far more votes than the opponents
g. Member of the Government
h. Worth to be repeated
i. You say something but you can't prove it
j. Something useful only for a particular purpose and nothing else
k. Department of the British government responsible for receiving, issuing and accounting for the money belonging to the State
l. Attitude preventing from harming or being angry with someone
m. People working in mines protesting against something
n. Opposite of success

Reading activities

Read the text carefully.

Hints. Complete the following statements, summarizing the passage.

Winston Churchill may be considered one of the key figure of the XX century because ...
Before entering Parliament in 1900, he ...
His political career is characterised by a series of controversial episodes. In fact, ...
However, when Hitler came to power in Germany in 1933, ...
After the war, Churchill ...

Post-reading activities

Research work.
The text you've just read mentions words like "Conservative", "Liberal", "M.P.", "P.M.", "Chancellor of the Exchequer", which clearly refers to politics. Find some information about the English political system. (You should focus on the following topics: Parliament and the two Houses; the Government and the Prime Minister; the role of the Queen.)

Research work.
Conservative v Labour: the two-party system has long characterised Britain's political life and is an essential element of the working of democracy. Outline the historical origins of the two most important English parties.

Listen to the tape and fill in the gaps with the missing words.

THE WAR AGAINST HITLER

On *May 19th, 1940 Winston Churchill became Prime Minister of Britain, a nation at war with Nazi Germany. Here he makes the first of many inspiring radio broadcasts:*

Winston Churchill:" I speak to you for the first time as _____ Minister in a solemn hour for the life of our country, of our _____ , of our allies and

above all of the cause of freedom. A tremendous _____ is raging in France and Flanders. The Germans, by remarkable combination of air bombing and heavily armoured tanks, have broken through the _____
defences north of the _____ Line and strong columns of their armoured vehicles, are ravaging the open country which, for the first day or two, was _____ defenders. For myself, I have invincible confidence in the French army and its _____ . Only a very small part of that splendid army has yet been heavily engaged and only a very small part of France has yet been _____ . There is good evidence to show that practically the whole of the specialised and mechanised forces of the _____ have been already thrown into the battle and we know that very heavy losses have been inflicted upon them. No officer or man, no brigade or _____ which grapples at close quarters with the enemy, wherever encountered, can fail to make a worthy contribution to the _____ results...
Having received His _____ Commission, I have formed an administration of men and _____ of every party and of almost every point of view. We have differed and _____ in the past, but now one bond unites us _____ to wage war until victory is won and never to surrender ourselves to _____ and shame, whatever the cost and the agony may be. If this is one of the most awe-striking periods in the long history of France and Britain, it is also, beyond doubt, the most _____ . Side by side, unaided except by their kith and kin in the great _____ and by the wide empires which rest beneath their shield, side by side, the British and French _____ have advanced to rescue not only _____, but mankind, from the foulest and most soul-destroying _____ which has ever darkened and stained the pages of history. Behind them... behind us, behind the _____ and fleets of Britain and France, gather a group of shattered states and bludgeoned races; the Czechs, the Poles, the _____, the Danes, the Dutch, the Belgians, upon all of whom the long night of barbarism will descend, unbroken even by a _____ of hope, unless we conquer, as conquer we must, as conquer we _____."

Warm-up activities

Discussion and revision.
Who was Winston Churchill? What happened in 1940? Reading the title can you imagine the content of Churchill's speech?

Vocabulary activity. Complete the definitions with the suitable words. Choose from the list below.

empire;   freedom;   to rage;   armoured;   tanks;   to break through; to

| ravage; | confidence; | loss; | to grapple at close quarters; | to quarrel; | to wage war; | awe-striking; | kith and kin; | shield; | to rescue; | foulest; | stained; | fleet; | shattered; | bludgeoned |

1. A(n) _____ is a group of nations controlled by a single country.
2. If a liquid _____ something, the thing becomes coloured or marked by the liquid.
3. To _____ means to struggle very closely against the enemy.
4. When you succeed in going beyond a barrier, you _____ it.
5. A _____ is a group of ships, organized together, for instance to fight in a battle.
6. If something _____, it breaks into a lot of small pieces.
7. _____ means to try and save someone from a dangerous situation.
8. A _____ is a military vehicle.
9. _____ means amazing, terrible, astonishing.
10. If you consider something horrible, you define it _____.
11. _____ someone means to hit him several times with a heavy object.
12. Troops or vehicle are _____ when have hard metal covering and protecting them from gunfire.
13. If you have _____ in me, you trust me.
14. When you have an argument with someone, you _____ with him.
15. _____ is an expression to indicate relatives.
16. If you do what you want, you have _____.
17. Ancient warriors used _____ to protect their bodies while fighting.
18. No longer having something is a _____.
19. If something is _____, it means it is almost completely destroyed.
20. When something powerful continues with great force and violence, we say it _____.
21. _____ means to start and continue a war or a campaign over a period of time.

Listening activities

Listen to the tape and complete the passage with the missing words.

After filling the gaps, check your answers with a partner. Then check them with the correct ones: Prime, Empire, battle, French, Maginot, without, leaders, invaded, enemy, division, general, Majesty's, women, quarrelled, all, servitude, sublime, dominions, peoples, Europe, tyranny, armies, Norwegians, star, shall.

Tasks. Now read the text again and say if the following statements are true (T) or false (F).

1. Winston Churchill speaks as a member of Parliament.
2. The Germans have already invaded France.
3. The Germans attacked using tanks and air power together.
4. According to Churchill, the situation in France is very critical.
5. The commission Churchill has formed is heterogeneous.
6. Churchill doesn't want to give it up, to surrender.
7. France and Britain struggle together against the enemy.
8. The Czechs, the Poles, the Norwegians, the Danes, the Dutch and the Belgians are all enemies of France and Britain.

Post-reading activities

This passage is written in 1st person singular: transform it into the 3rd person singular. Follow the example:

"I speak to you for the first time as Prime Minister in a solemn hour for the life of our country,..."

Winston Churchill speaks for the first time as Prime Minister in a solemn hour for the life of his country,

Angela T. Wesker

A lesson plan for vocabulary & grammar, sports and modal verbs

Content: Sports and modal verbs

Aims
• Ss will learn how to use modal verbs (must, mustn't, can) idea of language as SYSTEM;
• Ss will talk about sports and their rules — the idea of language as COMMUNICATION;
• Ss will learn new information about different sports and their rules - idea of language as CULTURE;
• Ss will learn how to behave by going/ doing/ playing sports idea of language as LEARNING;
• Ss will use two non-continuous texts to get, then classify and organize into categories, new information - idea of language as TEXT;

Level: A2 (CEFR- Companion Volume with New Descriptors); III secondaria di primo grado

Time: 2 hours

Methodology
Step 1. *(Activate the given)* Brainstorming activity at class level: What do you do in your spare time? What sports do you play? All words will be written on the board.

Step 2. T presents ss a list of several sports. *(Add the new)*

football	jogging	walking	ballet	weight-lifting	sailing
rugby	aerobics	skiing	swimming	karate	tennis	basketball
volleyball	judo	cricket	gymnastics	yoga	fishing	cycling

Step 3. T makes sure that all ss have understood each sport; if they don't, T explains unknown vocabulary which is integrated with the information of the brainstorming activity.

Step 4. T invites ss to classify the information into categories according to the specific characteristics of each sport. Examples are given, others will be added on ss' suggestions.

Use a ball	Are practised in the open air
Need specific equipment	**Are team sports**

Step 5. T gives ss the first activity. (*Assimilate the new to the given*)

Complete the following chart with the correct sport for each verb:

play	go	do

Step 6. T gives ss a list of rules of different sports. Ss read them in groups.*(Add the new)*

- ✓ You *must* have eleven players in each team.
- ✓ You *can* pass the ball to other players in your team.

✓ You *mustn't* touch the ball with your hand, except for one player in each team.
✓ To score a goal you *must* put the ball in the goal.
✓ You *mustn't* kick an opponent.
✓ You *can* touch the ball with your foot or your head.
✓ To play you *must* have two teams.

Step 7. T explains difficult words or expressions.

Step 8. Ss should now guess which sports the rules refer to.

Step 9. T tells ss to focus their attention on modal verbs, highlighting, in particular, the form of verbs following a modal verb (infinitive without "to"). *(Add the new)*

Step 10. Ss should do a second activity in small groups. *(Assimilate the new to the given)*

Complete the following chart with the corresponding rule:

Obligation to do something	Obligation not to do something	Permission to do something

Step 11. Final activity. Ss, in turn, think of possible rules and express them by using modal verbs. The class should guess which sport they refer to. T checks possible mistakes and helps ss. *(Accommodate the given to the new)*

A lesson plan for vocabulary, the human body and health

Content: The human body and its illnesses: talking about health

Aims
Language skills: Ss will create semantic fields about the human body and its illnesses.

Communication skills: Ss will listen to a dialogue and identify precise information. Ss will ask for and give personal information about health.

Cognitive skills: Ss will learn about the human body and its main diseases.

Level/target school and target class: B1 (from CEFR-Companion Volume with New Descriptors) - II liceo linguistico

Time: 2 hours

Teaching materials: A blackboard, photocopies, lab or a tape-recorder, a cassette

Methodology:
Step 1. Brainstorming activity at class level: the human body.

Step 2. Brainstorming activity at class level: human body illnesses.

Step 3. The T invites to list the information of the brainstorming activity according to the following categories: a)

parts of the human body; b) illnesses; c) expressions to ask a person how he/she is. Group work.

Step 4. Listening to a dialogue (i) once.

Step 5. The T invites the Ss to identify in the dialogue all information about health and the human body.

Step 6. Listening to the dialogue once again.

Step 7. The T invites the Ss to reorganize the information of the dialogue according to the previous categories. Group work.

Step 8. The T integrates further new information to give students a complete overview of health and illnesses.

Step 9. The T helps the Ss to understand the meaning of the new information with practical examples.

Step 10. The T invites the Ss to work in pairs and to make up a dialogue using the information of the previous activities. For instance, they can choose something wrong and act it out.

Step 11. The T goes from a pair to another to help Ss with difficulty, to control their speaking and to correct possible mistakes.

Step 11. As a final activity, the T gives Ss a T/F exercise (ii), presenting it as the instructions for the first aid in different situations. The Ss have to decide which ones are true and which ones are false. Individual activity. (If time is short, this activity may be given as homework.)

Neil and Polly meet on their way home from school.

Neil: Hello Polly.
Polly: Hello Neil.
Neil: What's the matter? You're very pale. Are you all right?
Polly: I don't feel too well. I've got a headache, my throat feels sore, my legs feel weak and I think I've got a temperature.
Neil: Perhaps you've got flu.

Polly: I hope not, but Amy and Emma have got it. Neil: Have you taken any aspirin or anything?

Polly: Not yet. I'm sorry, but I don't think I ought to go out this evening. I think I'd better stay at home.

Neil: Don't worry. You'd better have a hot drink and go to bed early. I'll come round and see you later if you like.

Polly: Thanks, it's very kind of you. And you, how are you?

Neil: Not too good, I'm afraid. I've just gone to visit my granny but it's so hot these days that I could even faint!

Polly: Oh, your grandmother, by the way, how is she?

Neil: She's recovering after the accident; two days ago she had been operated on her hips, but she still has got a sprained ankle and a terrible pain in her back.

Polly: Oh, poor thing. I'm very sorry, give her all my love.

1. In case of nose bleeding, tell the patient to pinch firmly the soft part of his/her nose for about ten minutes.	T	F
2. In case of nose bleeding, the patient can freely blow his/her nose.	T	F
3. In case of fainting, place the casualty on the ground with his/her arm raised.	T	F
4. In case of insect sting, never remove it with tweezers.	T	F
5. In case of fainting, sit the casualty up first before allowing him/her to stand up.	T	F
6. If you suspect the casualty has a broken leg, don't move him/her.	T	F
7. After the accident, the casualty may be given alcoholic drinks	T	F
8. ….	T	F

Angela T. Wesker

A lesson plan for grammar, the passive voice

Title: the passive voice

Class/level: 3^ istituto professionale per i servizi per l'enogastronomia e l'ospitalità alberghiera - B1 (from CEFR Companion Volume with New Descriptors)

National/school curriculum: Aims should come accordingly.
"SECONDO BIENNIO e QUINTO ANNO"
"Integrare le competenze professionali orientate al cliente con quelle linguistiche, utilizzando le tecniche di comunicazione e relazione per ottimizzare la qualità del servizio e il coordinamento con i colleghi; valorizzare e promuovere le tradizioni locali, nazionali e internazionali individuando le nuove tendenze di filiera. […] Lessico e fraseologia idiomatica frequenti relativi ad argomenti di interesse generale, di studio, di lavoro. Tecniche d'uso di dizionari, anche settoriali, multimediali e in rete. […] Produrre testi per esprimere in modo chiaro e semplice opinioni, intenzioni, ipotesi e descrivere esperienze e processi. […] Comprendere globalmente, utilizzando appropriate strategie, brevi messaggi radiotelevisivi e filmati divulgativi su tematiche note." (DPR 87/2010 & Linee Guida DM 5/2012)

Prerequisites:
From A2+ level of CEFR - Companion Volume with New Descriptors
"ONLINE INTERACTION GOAL-ORIENTED ONLINE TRANSACTIONS AND COLLABORATION: Can use formulaic language to respond to routine problems arising in online transactions (e.g. concerning availability of models and special offers, delivery dates, addresses, etc.); Can interact online with a supportive partner in a simple collaborative task, responding to basic instructions and seeking clarifica-

tion, provided there are some visual aids such as images, statistics, or graphs to clarify the concepts involved. ONLINE INTERACTION

ONLINE CONVERSATION AND DISCUSSION: can make short descriptive online postings about everyday matters, social activities and feelings, with simple key details; can comment on other people's online postings, provided that they are written in simple language, reacting to embedded media by expressing feelings of surprise, interest and indifference in a simple way; MEDIATING A TEXT RELAYING SPECIFIC INFORMATION IN WRITING: can relay in writing (in Language B) specific information contained in short simple informational texts (written in Language A), provided the texts concern concrete, familiar subjects and are written in simple everyday language."

Aims:
- Students will understand how to use the passive voice in a different context;
- Students will be able to write a recipe as a blog entry;

Materials needed:
- Strips of paper with active-voice sentences;
- Handout on reasons of how and when to use the passive voice;
- Flashcards that illustrate passive constructions;
- Magazine or newspaper articles.

Step 1. Review and anticipatory set. Activate the given.

In groups of three or four, students read the following recipes:

How to Make Tea	How to Make Lime Juice
• Boil a glass of water in a kettle/teapot. • When the water is still boiling, pour half a glass of milk into the boiling water. • Add two teaspoons of tea powder and sugar into the boiling content.	• Slice a lemon into two equal halves. • Squeeze the slices in a squeezer. • Collect the juice in a mug or in a half litre cup. • Add chilled water, sugar or salt and stir the mixture.

| • Stir the tea and serve hot. | |

The ss are invited to analyse the two texts from a grammatical point of underlining with different colours the verbs, the nouns, and the prepositions.

Step 2. Input and modelling. Add the new.
T writes the following sentence on the board:
Slice a lemon into two equal halves
and asks ss: what is the action? who is slicing a lemon? what happens to the lemon?

T then writes the following sentence on the board:
A lemon is sliced into two equal halves
asks students to work in small groups and decide on what the two sentences are different. Ss are given 10 minutes to answer. After that, t introduces the passive voice (verb be + past participle) using other examples. Then t explains the usage of "by whom" and the purpose of the passive voice. T can introduce the fact that we use the passive voice when we do not know who did a particular action or when it is not important.

Step 3. Elicit performance (practice) and provide feedback. Assimilate the new to the given.
In groups of three or four, T invites the ss to transform the two recipes using the passive voice. T monitors the correct use of verb tenses and the correct use of past participles.

Step 4. Enhance retention and transfer. Accommodate the given[9] to the new. After students appear to understand the new material they are given the opportunity to further apply or practise using the new information.

---

[9] Martin Dodman, notes from his methodology courses at the University of Pavia

Ss are given the following task:

> **You are a famous chef and you have a blog where you post your new recipes and answer your followers' questions giving advice. One of your followers has asked you how to make the authentic Italian *Tiramisù*. Write the ingredients they need, your suggested recipe and any tip you want. Use the passive voice when possible.**

Step 5. Enhance retention and transfer. Accommodate the given to the new. Homework. Ss are given a handout containing incomplete versions of different recipes, for example, "Chocolate Cake", "Pancakes", "Greek salad", "Tomato soup" "Bacon and Eggs" and "Fried chicken". The handout also contains a word bank to help ss decipher the recipe. At home, ss have to rewrite their correct recipe and to present it to the rest of the class.

A lesson plan for literature, Hamlet's monologue

Title: Hamlet's soliloquy

Class/level: III liceo linguistico- B1+/B2 (from CEFR- Companion Volume with New Descriptors)

National/school curriculum: Aims should come accordingly.

"SECONDO BIENNIO
Nell'ambito dello sviluppo di conoscenze relative all'universo culturale della lingua straniera, lo studente approfondisce aspetti relativi alla cultura dei paesi in cui si parla la lingua, con particolare riferimento agli ambiti sociale, letterario e artistico; legge, analizza e interpreta testi letterari con riferimento ad una pluralità di generi quali il racconto, il romanzo, la poesia, il testo teatrale, ecc. relativi ad autori particolarmente rappresentativi della tradizione letteraria del paese di cui studia la lingua; analizza e confronta testi letterari di epoche diverse con testi letterari italiani o relativi ad altre culture; analizza produzioni artistiche di varia natura provenienti da lingue/culture diverse (italiane e straniere) mettendoli in relazione tra loro e con i contesti storico-sociali; utilizza le nuove tecnologie dell'informazione e della comunicazione per approfondire argomenti di studio, anche con riferimento a discipline non linguistiche." (DPR 89/2010)

Prerequisites:
- Ss should know the main conventions of drama (e.g. what a play is, tragedy v comedy, what stage directions are, soliloquy v monologue...)
- Ss should know the main features of Elizabethan England from a cultural and historical point of view
- Ss should know the main aspects of Shakespeare's biography
- Ss should have very basic information about *Hamlet*

Aims:

LINGUISTIC

Mediating a text. expressing a personal response to creative texts (including literature): can give a clear presentation (or in some detail) of his/her reactions to a work, developing his/her ideas and supporting them with examples and arguments; can describe his/her emotional response to a work and elaborate on the way in which it has evoked this response. *Analysis and criticism of creative texts (incl. literature):* can evaluate the way the work encourages identification with characters, giving examples.

COGNITIVE
- Students will learn about Hamlet and his soliloquy
- Students will be able to demonstrate an understanding of the significance and influence of the context in which *Hamlet* was written
- Students will be able to articulate creative, informed and relevant responses to *Hamlet*
- Students will practise speaking through discussion and will practise writing advice

Materials needed
- Visual, auditory and kinaesthetic modalities (VAK) and cooperative learning will be preferred
- Paper worksheets are handed out in class.
- An interactive board

Time: 3 hours

Methodology:

Teachers should know their students' prior knowledge and learning experiences, their learning preferences, their attention spans, their ability to work independently or in groups. Special attention should be put on BES.

Step 1. Review. Stimulate recall of prior learning.

T can brainstorm the words "Shakespeare", "Hamlet" "tragedies" to revise the Elizabethan theatre and what ss already know about the play. Specific attention should be paid to words such as tragedy, Queen Elizabeth, the Globe Theatre, Denmark, the ghost… .

Step 2. Anticipatory set. Teachers should stir the students 'interest and create the urge to learn through piquing and intriguing questions in order to gain their attention.

To introduce the lesson, T asks ss if they are familiar with any quotations from Shakespeare. The famous verse "To be or not to be" has probably been heard: write it on the board.

T asks ss to discuss the following questions and monitor closely for any potential discussion. T asks for feedback from the open group and is sensitive to what learners say.

What makes you angry, sad or frustrated? Can you remember an episode in your life in which you felt particularly successful or unsuccessful?

Step 3. T explains what his/her aims (the ones listed in the planning section) are and what he/she's going to do in class with the students. "The more informed (and aware) learners are about language and language learning the more effective they will be at managing their own learning and at language learning." (Ellis and Sinclair)

Step 4. Input and modelling. Information gap task technique. Ss should work in pairs. Student A receives worksheet A containing Hamlet's thoughts in modern language. Student B receives worksheet B containing extracts from the original text. They should ask questions and discuss them in order to match the sentences.

An information gap task is a technique in language teaching where students are missing information necessary to complete a task or solve a problem and must communicate with their classmates to fill in the gaps. It is often used in communicative language teaching and task-based language learning.

Step 5. Input and modelling. Text presentation. Worksheet C contains the original text of Hamlet's monologue. T paraphrases to sort out syntax and explains difficult vocabulary. Specific questions on the monologue may be asked as the teacher's feedback.

Step 6. Enhance retention and transfer. Jigsaw activity. Worksheet F is handed out. Ss will learn how the play ends. It is done as a jigsaw reading activity in which at fist ss complete individual sentences then match them together. The purpose is to complete the summary of the play with the names of the characters. The original text is finally presented.

Step 7. Enhance retention and transfer. Discussing. Ss are asked to discuss the questions in worksheet D, which are also linked to the central themes of the play. It's an open class discussion which t monitors and clarifies doubts, especially with vocabulary.

After students appear to understand the new material they are given the opportunity to further apply or practise using the new information. This may occur in class or as homework, but there should be a short period of time between instruction and practice and feedback. This independent production makes the student responsible for his/her final learning outcomes. Activities can be rewriting notes, completing project assignments through peer interaction or group work. This is the student's authentic learning and he can finally say "I can do it".

Step 8. Enhance retention and transfer. Task-based language learning (TBLL). Writing. Ss are now asked to think about what advice they would give Hamlet and prepare written answers. Worksheet E is handed out. Ss are encouraged to use the structures such as "You should" and "If I were you". They should practise giving advice and opinions but in a controlled form.

Task-based language learning (TBLL) also known as task-based language teaching (TBLT) or task-based instruction (TBI) focuses on the use of authentic language and on asking students to do meaningful tasks using the target language.

<u>Step 9. Enhance retention and transfer.</u> <u>Mapping.</u> Ss are invited to draw mind maps or spider grams in order to organize all the materials (plot, themes, characters, motifs, symbols...) of the lesson(s). Having a neat concise review helps them study, remember and revise.
Free software to create mind maps are: CmapTools; XMind ot Mindomo Desktop.

<u>Step 10. Assess performance</u>. Teachers should assess to what extent the aims have been achieved. Teachers should ensure the assessment activity is directly and explicitly tied to the stated aims.

Quoting from the CEFR : "There are three concepts that are traditionally seen as fundamental to any discussion of assessment: validity, reliability and feasibility. [...] Validity is the concept with which the Framework is concerned. A test or assessment procedure can be said to have validity to the degree that it can be demonstrated that what is actually assessed (the construct) is what, in the context concerned, should be assessed, and that the information gained is an accurate representation of the proficiency of the candidates(s) concerned.

Reliability, on the other hand, is a technical term. It is basically the extent to which the same rank order of candidates is replicated in two separate (real or simulated) administrations of the same assessment. [...] Feasibility is particularly an issue with performance testing. Assessors operate under time pressure. They are only seeing a limited sample of performance and there are definite limits to the type and number of categories they can handle as criteria."

Example of assessment are:
- Completion activities (paragraphs, schemes, grids…)
- Multiple-choice questions
- T/F questions
- Open questions with a closed answer-

Possible links for <u>expansion</u>. Beyond literature.

T can show ss the scene of Hamlet's soliloquy taken from videos (films, recordings of drama versions). T can make ss pay attention to the specific features of a video (types of shot, soundtrack, costumes, setting, …) which also help information storage. On YouTube, you can find different versions (film, theatre, Oliver's, Gibson's, Burton's…)

Visual art. T can show ss famous pictures and paintings inspired by Shakespeare's play. For example Blake or Delacroix:

<u>Step 11. Post instructional reflection</u>. Teachers should take time to reflect upon the results and revise the lesson plan accordingly.

A lesson plan for a literary and historical period, the Puritan Age

Title: The Puritan Age

Time: 12 hours – 1 month

Target class/students' age: IV liceo linguistico /17-18 years old

Level: B2 (with reference to CEFR- Companion Volume with New Descriptors)

Analysis of the students' studying skills & learning styles:
- ♣ Levels of attention
- ♣ Needs and motivation (intrinsic, extrinsic, integral, instrumental)
- ♣ Learning styles (aural v visual)
- ♣ Types of intelligence (Gardner)
  - logical/mathematical;
  - verbal/linguistic;
  - naturalist;
  - intrapersonal;
  - interpersonal/social;
  - visual/spatial;
  - bodily/kinaesthetic;
  - musical/rhythmic)
- ♣ Maturity
- ♣ World knowledge and knowledge of & about English

Prerequisites:

LINGUISTIC
Level of English: B1+ (with reference to CEFR-Companion Volume)

COGNITIVE
Ss should know about the historical, social and literary context of the Anglo-Saxon period, the Middle Ages and the Renaissance.

Ss should be familiar with the main features of a poetic literary text

Ss should have the basic study skills to be able to read, understand and analyse a literary text under the teacher's guide (paraphrasing, taking and organizing notes…)

Ss should be familiar with specific technical terms used in poetry and what they consist of (denotation/connotation; figures of speech; meter; rhyme; poem; stanza…)

Ss should be familiar with certain tasks (filling charts, find quotations and examples, fill-in-the-gaps activities, matching exercises, cooperative work, task-based activities…)

Ss should be ready to find links with other school subjects to integrate and enrich their learning.

Ss should be familiar with creating mind maps using specific software

National curriculum. Aims should come accordingly.

"LINGUA. Lo studente acquisisce competenze linguistico-comunicative rapportabili al Livello B1.2 del Quadro Comune Europeo di Riferimento per le lingue. In particolare, lo studente comprende in modo globale, selettivo e dettagliato testi orali/scritti su argomenti diversificati; produce testi orali e scritti strutturati e coesi per riferire fatti, descrivere fenomeni e situazioni, sostenere opinioni con le opportune argomentazioni; partecipa a conversazioni e interagisce nella discussione, anche con parlanti nativi, in maniera adeguata sia agli interlocutori sia al contesto; elabora testi orali/scritti, di diverse tipologie e generi, su temi di attualità, letteratura, cinema, arte, ecc.; riflette sul sistema (fonologia, morfologia, sintassi, lessico, ecc.) e sugli usi linguistici (funzioni, varietà di registri e testi, aspetti pragmatici, ecc.), anche in un'ottica comparativa al fine di acquisire una consapevolezza delle analogie e differenze tra la lingua straniera e la lingua italiana; utilizza lessico e forme testuali adeguate per lo studio e l'apprendimento di altre discipline; riflette su conoscenze, abilità e strategie acquisite nella lingua straniera in funzione della trasferibilità ad altre lingue

CULTURA. Nell'ambito dello sviluppo di conoscenze relative all'universo culturale della lingua straniera, lo studente approfondisce aspetti relativi alla cultura dei paesi in cui si parla la lingua, con particolare riferimento agli ambiti sociale, letterario e artistico; legge, analizza e interpreta testi letterari con riferimento ad una pluralità di generi quali il racconto, il romanzo, la poesia, il testo teatrale, ecc. relativi ad autori particolarmente rappresentativi della tradizione letteraria del paese di cui studia la lingua; analizza e confronta testi letterari di epoche diverse con testi letterari italiani o relativi ad altre culture; analizza produzioni artistiche di varia natura provenienti da lingue/culture diverse (italiane e straniere) mettendoli in relazione tra loro e con i contesti storico-sociali; utilizza le nuove tecnologie dell'informazione e della comunicazione per approfondire argomenti di studio, anche con riferimento a discipline non linguistiche."
(from Indicazioni nazionali – DPR 89/2010)

Aims:

LINGUISTIC.

Improvement of communicative linguistic activities at level B2+. Oral and written production; aural and visual production; interaction;

MEDIATING A TEXT. NOTE-TAKING (LECTURES, SEMINARS, MEETINGS ETC.): can make accurate notes in meetings and seminars on most matters likely to arise within his/her field of interest. ANALYSIS AND CRITICISM OF CREATIVE TEXTS (INCL. LITERATURE): can compare two works, considering themes, characters and scenes, exploring similarities and contrasts and explaining the relevance of the connections between them; can give a reasoned opinion about a work, showing awareness of the thematic, structural and formal features and referring to the opinions and arguments of others; can evaluate the way the work encourages identification with characters, giving examples; can describe the way in which different works differ in their treatment of the same theme.

COGNITIVE/COMPETENCE

Ss will learn about the historical, social and literary context of the Puritan Age.

Ss will learn about John Milton and will be able to read and analyze a passage from Paradise Lost

Ss will learn about Isaac Newton and the Royal Society

Ss will learn about the human rights

Ss will be able to link the information presented with what he/she already has learnt in other subjects (Italian, Science, Art)

Ss will learn to develop media competence through a project on human rights

Materials needed:
- Worksheets of texts, images, and other materials are handed out in class from the class textbook or from the internet.
- An interactive board to present texts, images and other materials from the net.

Methodology:

Lesson 1 – 4 hours – the historical and social context

Step 1. Activate the given.
Warm-up. Ss are invited to discuss the role of the monarchy in England during the Middle Ages and the Renaissance, about the importance of Magna Charta.

Brainstorming activity: PURITAN/PURITANISM

All the ideas/words are written down on the interactive board. At the end, ss are invited to look up the unknown words in an online dictionary. Ss can enhance and consolidate their vocabulary.

On the interactive board, ss are presented a series of pictures to be matched with the corresponding captions (given in mixed order). Class activity.

1. *Charles I*
2. *Charles I is executed on 30th January 1649 before the Whitehall Banqueting House*
3. *Oliver Cromwell*
4. *A Puritan*

A

B

C

D

Step 2. Add the new. The historical and social context of the period, traditionally presented by the teacher in frontal lessons, is presented through cooperative work through the strategy of Jigsaw.

Groups are formed as follows. The texts can be taken from *Perfomer Heritage. From the Origins to the Romantic Age*, by Spiazzi/Tavella/Layton, Zanichelli Editore, 2016 or Amazing Minds. Wonderstanding. Volume 1, by Spicci/Shaw/Montanari, Pearson/Longman, 2017.

- Charles II and the clash with Parliament
- The Civil War and the Commonwealth
- The Puritan mind and society
- The Restoration of the Monarchy

Step 3. To assimilate the new to the given. Ss are asked to write notes of all information as a writing activity and for their later individual study.

Lesson 2 – 2 hours - John Milton's life

Step 1. Activate the given. Warm-up. To introduce the topic of the lesson, students are invited to say what they know about Satan. Class discussion.

Step 2. Add the new. Milton's life is presented on the workplace of the interactive board.

https://www.britannica.com/biography/John-Milton

Ss are invited to go to the board to find out the most important concepts (skimming - to quickly identify the main ideas of the text) and to underline the keywords marking them up with different colours (scanning – to search for the keywords and ideas). All concepts, words and ideas are discussed in class. This creates a constructive interaction thus meaningful learning.

Ss will intensively read the text at home and will use organize all information in a clear, accurate and meaningful way.

Lesson 3 – 3 hours – Milton's main work Paradise Lost and a text taken from it "Satan's speech"

Step 1. Activate the given. Warm-up. Students are shown pictures by Gustave Dorè and by William Blake illustrating Paradise Lost (these pictures will be lately analysed from an artistic point of view). Ss should predict the content of the poem and of the passage they are going to read.

Step 2. Add the new. The text is presented using the book or handouts.
The text is read aloud and the students listen. T focuses on pronunciation.

Text analysis follows: first comprehension (through questions) then analysis of meter (blank verse – Shakespeare), figures of speech (alliteration, run-on-lines…), and language.

Ss are then invited to read the introduction to the passage in their textbook. The teacher explains difficult concepts and adds further information.

Step 3. To assimilate the new to the given. Students are invited to draw mind a map or a spidergram in order to organize all the materials (including Milton's life and Paradise Lost) of the lessons in a clear, accurate and meaningful way. Having a neat concise review helps them study, remember and revise. Creating maps is particularly useful for SEN students. Free software to create mind maps are CmapTools, XMind, or Mindomo.

Lesson 4 – 2 hours – Isaac Newton and the Royal Society

Step 1. Activate the given. Warm-up. Ss are invited to look at the following images and to answer the following question: What do you associate the name of Isaac Newton to? Class discussion.

Step 2. Add the new. Information gap task. Students work in pairs. Each student receives the same text but with gaps in different positions. The text is taken from
https://answersingenesis.org/creation-scientists/profiles/sir-isaac-newton/?%2F=

The text must be completed at the end of the lesson to be studied at home. A mind map can be created to integrate the information learnt during the first lesson. (Assimilate the new to the given)

Step 3. Accommodate the given to the new.
Cross-curricular.
➢ Link with Italian literature.

Ss are invited to read from La Divina Commedia, Inferno by Dante Alighieri, canto XXXIV (lines 16-52), circle 9, Traitors the description of Dante's Lucifer to compare the two visions of Satan. Ss are asked triggering questions to help them put in evidence similarities and differences. Class discussion. At the end, ss can write two paragraphs about Dante's and Milton's Satan.

➢ Link with Science.

Ss are invited to integrate the information they have learnt about Newton with what they already know from Science about his scientific achievements. Ss are invited to give a definition of "scientific method" in English.

➢ Link with Art.

The illustrations by Dorè and Blake depicting Satan are precise representations from Paradise Lost. Ss can choose one illustration and describe it paying attention to the specific technical language used in Art. Biographical information can be added about Dorè and Blake. (To keep in mind when studying Blake as a Romantic poet).

 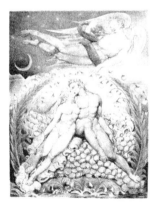

Ss can also be shown a photos of the front of St. Paul Cathedral (1), of Hampton Court Palace(2) and of Greenwich Royal Navy Hospital (3). With the help of the Art teacher, they should identify the main architectural elements (such as dome, pediment, relief), the materials employed, the organization of space… Terminology in Italian will be translated into English in class.

1

2

3

Step 4. Assess performance.

Continuous assessment. Ss are constantly monitored by the teacher. The teacher receives an ongoing feedback to modify his/her action in order to improve learning.

Summative assessment. It sums up attainment at the end of the whole project.

Achievement assessment: on specific aims of what has been taught. Open questions with a closed answer, multiple-choice questions, T/F questions, completion exercises, definition writing are just examples. SEN students can be tested through more structured activities and they have a longer time. If instructions can be an issue, they can be read aloud to students. DSA students can avoid written tests.

Proficiency assessment. Ss should develop the issue of Human Rights which is connected with the Puritan Age. Ss can update their learning and apply what they have studied in meaningful and "real world" contexts. Ss should create their own "projects" based on human rights. They can base their work on the history of human rights or find information where human rights are not respected nowadays. Ss are invited to use different applications or internet sites to develop their media competence. This assessment is particularly significant for

SEN students. They can also have a longer time to prepare the project work. Longer dead-line.

Angela T. Wesker

How to analyse an ESP text

International trade and indebtedness. Trade and development

With political independence, the LDCs inherited a structure of production and international trade that had largely been designed to serve the interests of the metropolitan powers, rather than those of the LDCs themselves.

They were heavily dependent on the production and export of a limited range of primary commodities (foodstuffs, fuels and industrial raw materials) going mainly to the developed capitalist economies. In many cases, that dependence has not yet been broken. At the present time, for example, coffee still represents approximately 90% of Burundi's recorded exports and 50% of Colombia's; copper accounts for more than 70% of Zambia's exports; cocoa represents more than 70% of Ghana's exports. Many other examples could be given.

The import structures of the LDCs were dominated by the importation of manufactured goods and intermediate inputs — durable consumer goods, machinery and transport equipment, chemicals, petroleum and so on. At independence, most trades was with the colonial 'mother country'.

Orthodox economists tended to argue that this structure of production and trade was consistent with the LDCs' comparative advantage and that they enjoyed significant gains from trade. The critics of this view, however, maintained that the gains from trade were more likely, for a variety of reasons, to be appropriated by the developed capitalist economies. The unequal exchange thesis, espoused by some neo-Marxists, went further and suggested that trade was actually carried out at the expense of the LDCs, reproducing the conditions of underdevelopment and poverty.

At the centre of the relationship between trade and development remains the controversy concerning the long-term (i.e. secular*) behaviour of the terms of trade of the LDCs. The commodity, or net barter, terms of trade are the ratio of the unit price of exports to the unit price of imports (a), and a deterioration in the index implies that a given volume of exports is exchanged for a smaller volume of imports.

The secular deterioration hypothesis is associated with the work of Hans Singer and Raul Prebisch. In its original form, it was based on the argument that in the developed economies strong trades unions could ensure that workers, rather than consumers, benefited from productivity gains, whereas in the LDCs, higher productivity led to lower prices, thus benefiting consumers in the developed economies. Associated with, although formally separate from, such arguments were the view that primary commodity export prices were highly unstable and prone to violent fluctuations, thus damaging the development of the LDCs.

*secular x long-term trend; note also cyclical = short-term fluctuation around the long-term trend.

The text *International trade and indebtedness. Trade and development* is at the level of FORMULATION.

GENRE
Academic economics textbook material; expositive type of text;

PURPOSE
The passage is addressed to university students of Economics with an intermediate level of English. It explains how international trade can be considered both as a continuation of the production system LDCs inherited from their mother countries after political independence or as a sort of change, marking the end of this structure of production. The passage also hints at the different theories upholding these considerations and at the possible consequent advantages or disadvantages for LDCs, for capitalist economies, for workers, for consumers etc.

DISCOURSE
Textual features
Anaphoric / cataphoric elements: the presence of reference to an element previously mentioned (anaphora) or to one to be mentioned below (cataphora). *Those of* ...(paragraph 1) stands for *the interests;*

Grammatical-logical operators (connectors): used to express a relation (cause/ effect, for instance) between two complex, recursively abstract ideas. *Rather than*...(paragraph 2); *however* (paragraph 4); *although* (paragraph 6);

Theme / rheme articulation: tendency to arrange sentences in such a way as to draw attention to what is communicatively more important and contributes to the development of communication. Many examples of linear articulation, typical of the English language: *the secular deterioration hypothesis* = theme 1 + *is associated...* = rheme 1 + *it* = theme2 + *was based...* = rheme2 (paragraph 6);

The structure of the narration clearly divided into paragraphs. The various linguistic acts have the following scheme of relations: ph. 1 = generalization; ph. 2 = addition + exemplification; ph. 3 = amplification; ph. 4 = addiction; ph. 5 = amplification; ph. 6 = addiction + amplification;

Linguistic function: referential;

Use of exemplification: it is often used in economics to help the understanding of a definition or an explanation, or to illustrate them. *For example* (paragraph 2); *i.e.* (paragraph 5);

Use of academic caution: in economics writing there is often the need to be tentative (i.e. to indicate less than 100 percent certainty'). The purpose is to show that a generalization is being made or that it is necessary to be cautious in making a statement or arriving at a conclusion: in other words, one is indicating a high degree of certainty, probability or possibility instead of total certainty. *Were more likely* (paragraph 4); *approximately* (paragraph 2); *tended to* (paragraph 4);

Pragmatic criteria v syntactic ones: a passive form, although more complex in grammatical terms, is textually simpler than the active one: *could be given* (paragraph 2);

Use of generalisation/depersonalisation: use of the passive voice without expressing the agent: *could be given* (paragraph 2);

Use of punctuation: many parenthetical sentences are used. *Associated with, although formally* (paragraph 6);

Syntactic features

The brevity of expression: the following devices are used to simplify the syntactic structure of sentences. E.g.: use of the *ing form* instead of a relative clause: *going* for *which used to go* (paragraph 2); *concerning* for *which concerns* (paragraph 5); use of the past participle instead of a relative clause: *espoused* for *which had been espoused* (paragraph 4); use of an adverb instead of a long coordinate sentence: *thus benefiting* (paragraph 6); use of a prefix *un-*: *unequal exchange thesis* for *the thesis supporting an exchange which is not equal* (paragraph 4); planning of the discourse, no redundancy;

Left-dislocation: e.g.: *the unequal exchange thesis* for *the thesis supporting an unequal exchange* (paragraph 4);

Use of nominalization: E.g.: *Coffee still represents approximately 90% of Burundi's recorded exports* (paragraph 2) for *As recorded, Burundi exports approximately 90% coffee;*

Lexical density: 40% of nouns and adjectives out of the total number of words (higher % of 'content words' out of the total number of words in the text);

Rather complex structure of noun phrases (due to nominalization, left-dislocation etc.). E.g.: *at the centre of the relationship between trade and development remains the controversy concerning the long-term behaviour* for *the controversy which concerns .the long-term behaviour remains at the centre of the relationship between trade and development* (paragraph 5);

Use of long sentences: E.g.: sentences of 5 lines (paragraph 6);

Syntactic parallelisms: *coffee still represents... copper accounts... cocoa represents...* (paragraph 2);

Morphological agreement: a singular subject agrees with a singular verb; the came for the plural. *They were...* (paragraph 2); *that dependence has...* (paragraph 2);

Use of verbal tenses: 12% of verb forms out of the total number of words; good proportion between main clauses and subordinate clauses;

Paragraph 1	*Inherited* (simple past active); *had been designed* (past perfect passive); *to serve* (infinite);
Paragraph 2	*Were dependent* (simple past active of to be + noun predicate); *going* (present participle functioning as a relative clause); *has not yet been broken* (present perfect passive); *represents, accounts, represents* (simple present active); *could be given* (present conditional passive);
Paragraph 3	*Were dominated* (simple past passive); *was* (past simple);
Paragraph 4	*Tended* (simple past active); *to argue* (infinite); *was consistent* (simple past of to be + noun predicate); *enjoyed, maintained* (simple past active); *were likely* (simple past of to be + noun predicate); *to be appropriated* (infinite of to be + noun predicate); *espoused* (reduced relative clause, simple past passive); *went, suggested* (simple past active); *was carried out* (simple past passive); *reproducing* (present participle functioning as a relative clause);
Paragraph 5	*Remains* (simple present active); *concerning* (present participle functioning as a relative clause); *are the ratio* (simple present of to be + noun predicate); *implies* (simple present active); *is exchanged* (simple present passive);
Paragraph 6	*Is associated* (simple present passive); *was based* (simple past of to be + noun predicate); *could ensure, benefited, led* (simple past active); *benefiting* (present participle functioning as a relative

| | clause); *associated* (reduced relative clause, simple past passive); *was the view, were unstable...*(simple past of to be + noun predicate); *damaging* (present participle functioning as a relative clause); |

Note. The simple present time is used to express factuality, general truths; the simple past is used for past events; the present perfect is used to relate events to each other; The **passive** is frequently used, being more impersonal and, therefore, more suitable for academic writing; the agent is rarely expressed. Non-finite (present participle or infinite functioning as reduced relative clauses) are used to make to text simpler and more synthetic.

These features render the passage:

Coherent: the relation among the meanings of the various sentences exists on the basis of external information (economics). LDCs = less developed countries (paragraph 1);

Cohesive: there are inferential relations referring to words and expressions that help to link ideas between sentences and paragraphs.

Lexical features (TERMINOLOGY/VOCABULARY)

Transparency of meaning: one word/one meaning (the denotative aspect is privileged; the meaning of words is independent of the context). E.g.: *secular =. long-term* in Economics writing; *worldly, centennial* in general English;

Specific economics terminology: *primary commodity* (paragraph 2); *durable consumer goods* (paragraph 3); *net barter* (paragraph 5);

Academic formal vocabulary: *consistent of* (paragraph 4); *espoused* (paragraph 4); *prone to* (paragraph 6); *maintained* (paragraph 4);

Vocabulary of Latin origin: *durable* (paragraph 3); *ratio* (paragraph 5); *index* (paragraph 5); *volume* (paragraph 5); *ar-*

gument (used with the meaning of series or reasons, more formal, paragraph 6);

Collocations: two or more expressions or words generally occurring together in a sentence. *To be consistent with* (paragraph 4); *to enjoy gains* (paragraph 4); *at the expense of* (paragraph 4); *to be prone to* (paragraph 6); *to espouse a thesis* (paragraph 4);

Presence of synonyms: *hypothesis* (paragraph 6) / *argument* (paragraph 6) > economics;

Presence of antonyms: *import* (paragraph 3) / *export* (paragraph 4) > economics;

Presence of acronyms: *LDCs* (paragraph 1) for less developed countries;

Presence of hypernyms: *chemicals, machinery, transport equipment* (paragraph 3);

Presence of hyponyms: *cocoa; coffee; copper* (paragraph 2)

Use of metaphor: *went further* (paragraph 4) for *said more* (no real movement)

Compounding/pre-modification: *trade unions* = noun + noun compound (paragraph 6); v *international trade* = pre-modification of classification (the most frequent in the passage) (paragraph 1); *secular deterioration hypothesis* (paragraph 6); *manufactured goods* (paragraph 3);

Post-modification: *commodity terms of trade* (paragraph 5);

Derivational processes: *under/develop/ment* = preposition (prefix) + verb + suffix (paragraph 4); *small/er* = adjective + suffix (paragraph 5); *formal/ly* = adjective + suffix (paragraph 5); *un/stable* = prefix + adjective (paragraph 6);

A lesson plan for ESP, economics

Target school: istituto tecnico indirizzo AFM/liceo scientifico

Target class: V year

Level: B2 (with reference to CEFR- Companion Volume with New Descriptors)

National curriculum. Aims should come accordingly.
SECONDO BIENNIO E QUINTO ANNO
"Redigere relazioni tecniche e documentare le attività individuali e di gruppo relative a situazioni professionali individuare e utilizzare gli strumenti di comunicazione e di team working più appropriati per intervenire nei contesti organizzativi e professionali di riferimento. […] Strategie per la comprensione globale e selettiva di testi relativamente complessi, scritti, orali e multimediali. Caratteristiche delle principali tipologie testuali, comprese quelle tecnico-professionali; fattori di coerenza e coesione del discorso. Lessico e fraseologia idiomatica frequenti relativi ad argomenti di interesse generale, di studio o di lavoro; varietà espressive e di registro. […] Distinguere e utilizzare le principali tipologie testuali, comprese quelle tecnico-professionali, in base alle costanti che le caratterizzano. […] Comprendere idee principali e specifici dettagli di testi relativamente complessi, inerenti la sfera personale, l'attualità, il lavoro o il settore di indirizzo." (DPR 88/2010 – DM 4/2012)

Teaching materials: photocopies of the text and of the relative activities;

Prerequisites:
Linguistic
Receptive: B2 visual reception (reading);

Cognitive

Angela T. Wesker

General knowledge of some of the most important aspects of Economics from both a historical and a contemporary point of view: the meaning of economic development; various economic theories (e.g.: Karl Marx's v Capitalism); definition of urbanisation, unemployment, and industrialization; the role of technology in development.

Aims:
Linguistic.
Improving visual reception (reading).

Cognitive.
Give practice in the English that is commonly used in economics studies (many students are going to study Economics at University), including grammatical features, vocabulary, language functions, study skills and use of data.

Give an example of the kind of language students must face in their future economic studies.

Pre-reading activities

1. Match the words on the right with their corresponding explanation on the left.

   1) LDCs;
   2) Commodities;
   3) Capitalist economies;
   4) Consumer;
   5) Orthodox;
   6) Underdevelopment;
   7) Long-term;
   8) Ratio;
   9) Deterioration;
   10) Trade Union;
   11) Fluctuations;
   12) Neo-Marxist;

a) something that is sold for money, such as food, machinery or clothing.
b) something accepted or believed by most people.
c) something that will continue for a long time in the future.
d) when a rate, a speed or a cost is irregular or changes a lot.
e) worsening of conditions.
f) organization of workers that represents them and has the aim of improving such things as the working conditions, pay, and benefits of its members.
g) less developed countries (India, for instance).
h) a person who buys things and uses services.
i) a country in which property, business, and industry are owned by private individuals and not by the state, and in which companies are run in competition with each other in order to make a profit.
l) without modern industries or proper social organization and usually with a lower standard of living.
m) a relationship between two amounts or measurements, showing how much greater one is than the other when they are compared.
n) related to Marxism, a political philosophy based on the writings of Karl Marx.

Reading activities

The following statements are based on the information in the passage. Decide if they are true (T) or false (F):

1. The structure of production and international trade that LDCs inherited when they became independent was generally to their advantage.
2. LDCs were greatly dependent on primary products for exports and on importing manufactures goods and intermediate inputs.
3. Some economists have agreed that LDCs have a comparative advantage in trade and have therefore benefited from it.
4. A worsening of the index of export and import prices for LDCs suggests that a smaller quantity of imports will be received in exchange for a given quantity of exports.
5. The secular deterioration theory was based on the argument that in the developed economic productivity gains benefited workers while in LDCs higher productivity benefited consumers in the developed economies.
6. The view was held that variations in the export prices of primary products were to the advantage of the LDCs.

2. Answer the following questions, obtaining information from the passage.

1. Give three examples of the current reliance on LDCs on primary products for exports.
2. What are the arguments which suggest that there were no advantages to be gained by LDCs from their structure of production and trade?
3. Give a definition of the net barter terms of trade.

3. Refer back to the text and find synonyms or expressions with the same meaning for the words listed below. The first one has been done for you:

a. Exchange: (line 26) barter
b. Unsteady:
c. Owing money:
d. Liable:
e. Theory-
f. Long-lasting:
g. Supported, adopted:
h. The advantage of, profit:
i. Causing loss to, with the sacrifice of:

Post-reading activities

Complete the passage below, a summary of the text you've read, with the words in the box below:

Workers, underdevelopment, higher, advantage, price, countries, main, exports, imports, state.

Although politically independent, LDCs' economic structure was to the _____ of the developed capitalist countries, with which they used to trade.
Some economists _____ that LDCs benefited from this trade; others, on the contrary, consider it the _____ cause of LDCs' _____ and poverty. Still controversial remains the ratio between the _____ of exports

and the price of imports: the situation worsens if _____ exceed (deterioration
hypothesis). This theory also maintains that in the developed economies productivity gains benefited _____, while in LDCs it's consumers in the developed _____ countries to be benefited by _____ productivity.

Assessment

The following exercise is used as an on-going activity to check students' comprehension. Choose the correct answer:

1. When did the LDCs inherit a structure of production and international trade designed to serve the interests of the metropolitan powers?
    a. After WWI;
    b. With political independence;
    c. In 1961;

2. What are the primary commodities?
    a. Foodstuffs, fuels and industrial raw materials;
    b. Game;
    c. Electronic devices;

3. The import structures of LDCs were dominated by ...
    a. Manufactured goods and intermediate inputs;
    b. Primary commodities;
    c. Foodstuffs only;

4. Who argued that LDCs enjoyed significant gains from trade with their mother countries?
    a. Neo-Marxists
    b. Hans Singer and Raul Prebish
    c. Orthodox economists

5. How do we call the ratio unit price of exports to the unit price of imports?
    a. Net barter
    b. Deterioration index
    c. Long-term behaviour
6. What implies a deterioration in the index?

a. A given volume of imports is exchanged for a smaller volume of exports
   b. A given volume of exports is exchanged for a smaller volume of imports
   c. A smaller volume of exports is exchanged for a bigger volume of imports

7. According to the secular deterioration hypothesis, who benefited from productivity in the developed countries?
   a. Consumers;
   b. Trade unions;
   c. Workers;

8. What is unstable and prone to violent fluctuations?
   a. Primary commodity import prices;
   b. Primary commodity lower prices;
   c. Primary commodity export prices;

A lesson plan for ESP, tourism

Title: Italy and its cultural and artistic treasures

Class/level: V Istituto tecnico per il turismo - B2 (from CEFR – Companion Volume with New Descriptors);

National/school curriculum:
"Utilizzare i linguaggi settoriali delle lingue straniere previste dai percorsi di studio per interagire in diversi ambiti e contesti di studio e di lavoro; riconoscere il valore e le potenzialità dei beni artistici e ambientali, per una loro corretta fruizione e valorizzazione; individuare ed utilizzare le moderne forme di comunicazione visiva e multimediale, anche con riferimento alle strategie espressive e agli strumenti tecnici della comunicazione in rete;" (DPR 88/2010 – allegato A)

Prerequisites:
- Ss should have basic grammar information to be able to understand texts and materials in English;
- Ss should have basic knowledge of the main aspects of tourism and its vocabulary;
- Ss should have basic computer skills;

Aims:
- Students will learn how to use precisely the technical jargon of art;
- Students will learn about city maps and their facilities;
- Students will be able to create possible cruise itineraries;
- Students will understand and identify target clients for art cities (interests, expectations…);
- Students will be able to create the travel offer (accommodation, itinerary, activities) as an email or letter;
- Students will learn how to examine authentic material to create their own personal work;

Materials needed:
- Informative materials from the internet or from paper catalogues concerning art cities and possible itineraries;
- Paper letters or emails advertising a cruise (promotional material);
- Computer lab;

Methodology:

Step 1. Review. Stimulate recall of prior learning. T should check if ss know what a brochure, a catalogue, a newsletter is; the difference between check-in and check-out; the different kinds of accommodation; what a cruise consists of; simple strategies of promotion. Prior learning can be recalled by asking questions.

Step 2. Anticipatory set. Teachers should stir the students' interest and create the urge to learn through piquing and intriguing questions in order to gain their attention.

T shows ss the following images and brainstorms their ideas. Ss may recognize the cities: t invites ss to use their English names. Ss may identify the main monuments of these cities.

Lesson Planning in an EFL Class - Concorso a cattedra 2020

T can help ss to organize their random ideas with a mind map containing all information. T also explains what his/her aims are and what he/she's going to do in class with the students. T explains ss how they will work in class.

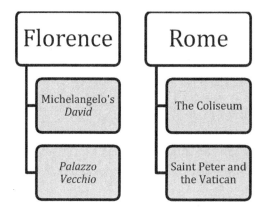

Step 3. Input and modelling. Teachers should select and develop the appropriate teaching and learning resources, providing students with learning guidance. Teachers should use materials to show students examples of what is expected to be the end product of their work. Thanks to the internet t can use authentic material and ask ss to work on real tasks.

https://www.italyguides.it/en

The site *ItalyGuides* presents a rich collection of more than 200 virtual panoramas of Italy's most famous art city monuments. SS can explore them 360° and each of them comes with text written by history of art professionals. *ItalyGuides.it* also provides free audio guides download (for iPod or mp3), video in high definition (HDTV), google maps and more than 3000 photos in our photo galleries. The site is very useful to get authentic, up-to-date information and materials.

The four cities ss will analyse are Rome, Florence, Venice, and Milan. For each city, ss in pairs choose a monument (for example the Roman Coliseum for Rome or Michelangelo's *David* for Florence). Each pair should read and summarize the text on the internet. Then they have to present the class the monument and has to hand out a written copy of the summary. At the end of the activity, each student has worked on four specific monuments for every art city and has received information about other important monuments to have a complete overview of each city. This activity is an example of jigsaw.

Step 4. Input and modelling. Model art itinerary and vocabulary. Ss should read the model itineraries of Florence on the web page

http://www.firenzeturismo.it/en/informazioni-utili-2/itinerariafirenze-2/in-48-ore-2.html
http://www.firenzeturismo.it/en/informazioni-utili-2/itinerariafirenze-2/in-72-ore-2.html
http://www.firenzeturismo.it/en/informazioni-utili-2/itinerariafirenze-2/itinerariatema-2.html

The monuments listed shouldn't be new to the ss because of the previous activity. On the map, ss should draw the different spots of the itinerary. T should stress the importance of logically ordering the spots to visit.

From this text and from the summaries of the previous activity ss can make a list of all technical jargon of art they have found (*façade, fresco…*). Ss write the word in alphabetical order with the corresponding definition.

Step 5. Input and modelling. Itinerary.
T presents another itinerary of Florence which includes transportation, accommodation, meals and other services.

Class discussion. Ss are invited to express their own opinions about the offer. T underlines the main point of a promotional itinerary (costs, what is included, insurance et.) T writes a series of questions (whose answers may have already been elicited from the discussion) to fix the main elements.

Step 6. Elicit performance (practice) and provide feedback. Now ss are ready to integrate the information for the two previous activities, i.e. artistic information about what to see and practical information. Close monitoring and direction of the students are necessary as they practise the whole task for the first time independently of each other. In small groups.

Step 7. Enhance retention and transfer. Promoting your itinerary. Ss are now asked to write a personal promotional letter to promote the itinerary they have created. They need to be as convincing as possible.

Step 8. Enhance retention and transfer. Another activity that can help ss to enhance retention and transfer could be that of creating an animated video promoting the itinerary chosen. This also increases the ss's motivation.

www.goanimate.com

Step 9. Assessment and evaluation. Teachers may decide to evaluate the written production of their students.

A lesson plan for cross-curricular learning

Target class/level: III year of scuola secondaria di primo grado; A2 (from CEFR – Companion Volume with New Descriptors);

Time of realization: 8 lessons (60' each);

Prerequisites
Linguistic
Receptive: visual reception at A2 level (reading).

Cognitive
Basic knowledge of the topics of the teaching unit (The British Empire, Gandhi and modern India) in Ll, dealt with other subjects (History and Geography);
Familiarity with certain tasks (wh-questions, T/F exercises, interpreting maps/pictures/images);

Aims
Linguistic
Practise and improvement of communicative linguistic activities.
Productive. Oral(speaking): expressing critical opinions supported by a written text; written (writing): writing short compositions;
Receptive. Visual reception: (reading): reading civilization texts; "reading" maps, photographs, and pictures about the topics of the T.U.;
Interactive. Oral interaction: discussing with other people;

Cognitive
Knowledge of the main features of the British Empire;
Knowledge of the main biographical aspects of Gandhi;
Knowledge of certain characteristics of the modern Indian society;
Integrating information from different subjects (History, Art, French...)

Teaching materials: hand-outs (photocopies) of texts, images, pictures, activities etc.; the multimedia lab;

Methodology

Lesson 1

Step 1. A pre-reading activity is done in class as a warm-up to make students "activate the given", what they already know about the subject.

1. Look at the following timeline:

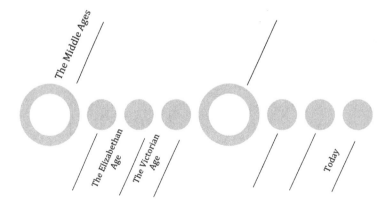

Now read the names of the characters you find below and write the name in the timeline:

Napoleon (1789 - 1821) ...
Donald Trump...
Christopher Columbus (1451 - 1502)
Queen Victoria ...
The Beatles (1960 - 70) ...
Hitler (1889 - 1945) ...
William Shakespeare (1563 - 1616) ...
Robin Hood ...

Step 2. The following text is read in class. The teacher explains difficult vocabulary items and information. Maps and images support comprehension.

THE BRITISH IN INDIA

During Queen Victoria's reign (1837-1901), British Empire extended over all five continents.

India was under the British control since 1857, for ninety years: in 1876 Queen Victoria became Empress of India.

India was dominated by military strength and strict rule. Farmers were obliged to cultivate tea, sugar, and cotton as the British needed these products for their commercial interests. This destroyed the traditional Indian agriculture and the country began to suffer poverty and famine.

However, colonial rule was not entirely negative. The British

built railways, roads and ports, created schools and hospitals and introduced the English culture and language.

At the beginning of the XX century, the colonies were tired of British rule and wanted independence. India reached it thanks to Gandhi's protests.

Step 3. A comprehension activity is given as homework.

1. Decide if the following sentences are true (T) or false (F):
a. Queen Victoria's reign lasted 64 years.
b. Canada was under British control.
C. In 1897 Queen Victoria became Empress of Australia.
d. India cultivated flowers Britain exported all over the world.
e. The destruction of Indian agriculture caused poverty and famine.
f. Railways, schools, ports were built by the British.
g. Gandhi's activity contributed to Indian independence.

Step 4. Students are shown the following image with the purpose of developing possible cross-curricular connections with art and to give them a visual representation of the information read in the passage. The teacher explains the picture by saying:

"This image represents Queen Victoria presenting the Bible to an Indian Prince. This shows how strictly the British ruled: they wanted to impose the English culture, cancelling the Indian religion. Art becomes a device to explain and justify the British power and to show the force of their rulers. The imperial values are perfectly exalted."

On page 71: Queen Victoria presenting the Bible in the Audience Chamber at Windsor. Painted in 1861 by T. Jones Barker.

This works as a cross-curricular activity with ART.

Lesson 2

Step 5. Before reading the passage, the students have to show what they already know about Gandhi through the following warm-up activity.

1. What do you already know about Gandhi? Which of these pieces of information is correct? Tick the correct piece of information.

European leader	Indian leader
Christian	Hindu
In favour of peace	In favour of war
Used violent methods	Used non-violent methods
Born in the 19" century	Born in the 20" century
Assassinated	Still living today

Step 6. Then the passage is read in class so that students can understand it completely (content and vocabulary).

GANDHI

Gandhi, a young lawyer during his stay in South Africa (1894 - 1914)

A life for peace (1869 - 1948)
Gandhi was born in India, on October 2, 1869. His family belonged to the caste of traders. When he was only 14, he married a girl of his age. Her name was Kusturbai.

Eight years later, he took a degree in law at London University. After that, he lived in South Africa for twenty years, where he fought for the civil rights of Indian emigrants and was sent to prison for his struggles against apartheid.

When World War One broke out in 1914, Gandhi went back to India. In 1914 Gandhi was appointed President of the India National Congress. He promoted many campaigns of civil disobedience to force the British to leave his country.

One of his most famous non-violent campaigns became known as the "March of the Salt". In 1930 Gandhi and his followers began to gather salt without paying taxes to the Imperial authorities.

After his liberation from prison, Gandhi began a series of hunger strikes to convince the British government to grant more rights to the Indian people.

Gandhi in 1930 during the "March of the Salt"

From 1940 to 1944 the Mahatma was in prison again because he had requested the British to leave India.

He was finally freed because he had malaria.

Anglo-Indian newspapers talking about Gandhi's release from prison

After many years of hunger-striking, civil disobedience and long negotiations with the British government, on August 15, 1947, the British King renounced the title of Emperor of India and India became independent.

About 5 months later, on January 30, 1948, Mahatma Gandhi was murdered by a Hindu extremist.

Angela T. Wesker

Gandhi's funeral procession

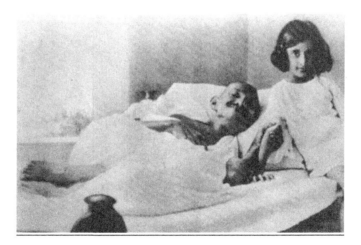

Gandhi on his 21st day of hunger- strike. The girl next to him is Indira Gandhi. She later became President of the Republic of India.

Gandhi's ideas

The non-violent ideas of Gandhi spread all over the world. During his life, he became very popular in Europe and in North America.

Lesson Planning in an EFL Class - Concorso a cattedra 2020

Above left: Gandhi outside 10, Downing Street; right: Gandhi with women textile workers in Darwen, Lancashire

Step 7. These comprehension activities are given as homework and corrected in class during the following lesson.

1. Answer the following questions:

a) What are Gandhi's origins?
b) Where did he take his degree?
c) What did Gandhi do when he was in South Africa?
d) What did he do when he went back to India?
e) Why was one of Gandhi's most famous campaigns called the "March of the Salt"?
f) Why did Gandhi begin a series of hunger-strikes?
g) Why was he in prison again?
h) When did the British King renounce the title of Emperor of India?
i) What did this act mean for India?
j) How did Gandhi die?

2. Read Gandhi's biography and complete the chart with the main information:

Name
Place of birth
Date of birth
Caste of family
Name of wife
Date of marriage

Education
Period in South-Africa
Key ideas
Date of the "March of the Salt"
Date of death

3. The passage contains some words you may find difficult. This exercise will help you understand their meaning. Complete the following sentences with the suitable word:

| trader   spread   appointed   gather   degree |
| break (broke) out   murdered   freed   fight (fought)   grant |

a. Soldiers _____ against the enemy.
b. At the University you may get a _____
c. A person who buys and sells things is a _____
d. _____ means killed in a violent way.
e. _____ may be translated in Italian with "raccogliere".
f. _____ is the opposite of imprisoned.
g. We say that, for instance, a war _____ if it begins violently and suddenly.
h. To be _____ means to be chosen by somebody for a particular purpose.
i. If you _____ something to somebody else, you surely give it to him/her.
j. _____ may be translated in Italian with "diffondersi".

Step 8. The teacher asks students to carry out the following activity, in pairs or in small groups, in the multimedia lab. Students will surf the net to find information both visual and written. The teacher will help students with the most difficult written resources. This activity has the purpose of making students find a possible connection with the SECOND FOREIGN LANGUAGE studied.

4. Gandhi played an important role in the history of Great Britain. Can you find another character with the same importance for the history of France/Spain/Germany? Surf the net to find information. Then write a short composition.

Lesson Planning in an EFL Class - Concorso a cattedra 2020

3 lesson

Step 9. The following text is read and explained in class.

INDIA: THE IMMENSE COUNTRY

STATISTICS
Area: 3,287 263 km^2
Population: 1,352,642,280 2nd most populated country in the world after China
Capital: New Delhi; largest city: Mumbai; other cities: Calcutta, Madras)
Government: Federal Parliamentary Constitutional Republic
Currency: Rupee
Languages: Hindi, English, Urdu and 13 other official languages
Religions: Hinduism (83%), Islam (14%), Roman Catholic (3%), Sikh (2%)
Main occupations: textile industry, iron metallurgy, agriculture, oil refineries etc.
Main exports: textiles, fish, tea, machinery, precious stones, iron minerals etc.
Main imports: machinery, chemical products, pharmaceuticals, foodstuff.

Step 10. The students have to do the following activity. T This activity is cross-curricular with GEOGRAPHY.

5. Read on your geography textbook what it says about India.
Integrate other information you can find on the internet. Finally, create a conceptual map like the one below.

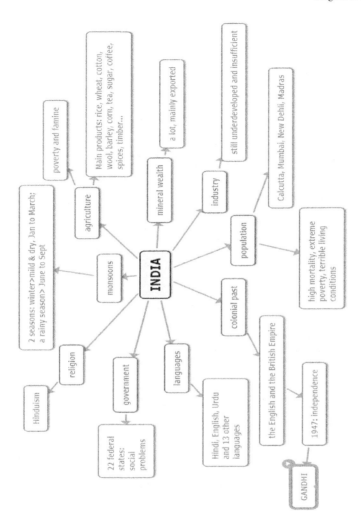

Step 11. In order to assess the Teaching Unit, the teacher considers the in-class participation of students, which gives evidence of the skills and thinking processes they implemented during the T.U., such as, for instance, cooperation, critical thinking, analysis, and synthesis…

Through a final oral test, students may demonstrate their ability to identify possible connections among subjects as well as effective learning.

Glossary of Educational Linguistics

Ability vs Skill[10]

A communicative task requires several (linguistic) skills coming together, integrated, articulated with each other, feeding on each other, and rendering a (communicative) ability. Linguistic skills are teaching strategies that require the receptive/productive manifestation of **isolated** linguistic aspects without a real communicative purpose, other than the practice of these same linguistic aspects. By contrast, a communicative ability will promote a **global** analysis of the context, with all its variables, which will also integrate those linguistic aspects that were isolated because of context. This type of approach is most desirable since it contributes to enabling language users, to both understand and produce language. Skills can be receptive i.e. listening and reading. Learners do not need to produce language to do these, they receive and understand it. Speaking and writing are productive or active skills.

Achievement vs proficiency vs diagnostic tests

Achievement tests evaluate a learner's understanding of a specific course or study programme. Proficiency tests measure a learner's level of language. Diagnostic tests identify areas learners need to work on.

Acquisition vs Learning[11]

One of the 5 hypotheses of Krashen's Theory of Second Language Acquisition. 'Acquisition' is the product of a subconscious process very similar to the process children undergo when they acquire their first language. "Learning" is the product of formal

---

[10] WIDDOWSON, H. G. (1998) Teaching Language as Communication. OUP. Oxford
[11] Krashen, Stephen D. Principles and Practice in Second Language Acquisition. Prentice-Hall International, 1987 and Krashen, Stephen D. Second Language Acquisition and Second Language Learning. Prentice-Hall International, 1988.

instruction and it comprises a conscious process which results in conscious knowledge 'about' the language, for example, knowledge of grammar rules. A deductive approach in a teacher-centred setting produces "learning", while an inductive approach in a student-centred setting leads to "acquisition".

Acronym see Word formation

Accuracy vs Fluency
Accuracy refers to how correct learners' use of the language system is, including their use of grammar, pronunciation, and vocabulary. Fluency refers to how well a learner communicates meaning rather than how many mistakes they make in grammar, pronunciation, and vocabulary.

Affective factors
They are emotional factors that influence learning. They can have a negative or positive effect. Negative affective factors are called affective filters and are an important idea in theories about second language acquisition.

(The) Affective Filter Hypothesis
One of the 5 hypotheses of Krashen's Theory of Second Language Acquisition. When the filter is 'up' it impedes language acquisition. Krashen claims that learners with high motivation, self-confidence, a good self-image, a low level of anxiety and extroversion are better equipped for success in second language acquisition. Low motivation, low self-esteem, anxiety, introversion, and inhibition can raise the affective filter and form a 'mental block' that prevents comprehensible input from being used for acquisition.

Affixes
They are groups of letters that are added to the beginning or the end of words to make new words. Prefixes go at the beginning of words and often change meaning, whilst suffixes go at the end of words and often change the kind of word (e.g. from verb to noun, or noun to adjective, etc.).

Allomorphs

They are different forms of the same morpheme or basic unit of meaning. These can be different pronunciations or different spellings. There are three allomorphs of the morpheme -s in English. Compare the sound of the -s in 'cats', 'dogs' and 'foxes'.

Allophones see Phonemes

Anaphora vs Cataphora

In text, these terms define two mechanisms of cohesion. Anaphora is a reference to a previous section of the text; cataphora is a reference to information that has yet to appear.

Anchoring

It is a technique used to manage emotional states in Neuro-Linguistic Programming. It involves setting up an association with a desired mental state such as happiness or calm by creating anchor stimuli to that state. Anchoring is one of the various NLP techniques which have applications not only in terms of managing thinking and feeling but also as classroom activities to support other learning aims.

Anticipation

It consists of predicting what can appear in a text by operating based on the situation, of the part of the text that has already been understood, of the paratext, of the knowledge of the world. It may be stimulated with the elicitation activities and is strengthened with techniques such as cloze, dictation, joints.

Antonym

It is a word which means the opposite of another word.

Approach

It is a way of looking at teaching and learning. Underlying any language teaching approach is a theoretical view of what language is, and of how it can be learnt. An approach gives rise to methods, the way of teaching something, which uses classroom activities or techniques to help learners learn.

Aspect

It is information described by a verb that is not related just to tense and time. For example, the aspect shows whether an action is unfinished or not. It can be compared to tense, which refers to the verb's past or present form, and time, which is whether the verb refers to past, present or future. In English, aspects include the simple, the continuous and the perfect.

Assessments

There are <u>continuous assessments</u> when you are assessing aspects of learners' language throughout their course and then producing a final evaluation result from these assessments. Continuous assessment often provides a more accurate and complete picture of the learner's level and has a positive impact on learning. <u>Formative assessment</u> is the use of assessment to give the learner and the teacher information about how well something has been learnt so that they can decide what to do next. It normally occurs during a course. <u>Summative assessment</u> evaluates a learner's progress up to that point and provides a summary of where they are. It can be compared to formative assessment, which gives the teacher and learner helpful information for future work. <u>Formal assessments</u> use formal tests or structured continuous assessment to evaluate a learner's level of language. It can be compared to <u>informal assessments</u>, which involve observing the learners' performance as they learn and evaluating them from the data gathered.

ASTP

Army Specialized Training Program. It was a project carried out by the American army during the Second World War to prepare officers and soldiers who were to be employed in the nations gradually occupied by the Allies. Since the Reading Method had dominated the United States for at least two decades, the Americans lacked the oral dimension in the foreign language and implemented the ASTP with great commitment of resources and people. The program was based on an intensive method, which in part took up the concepts of the direct method, in part laid the foundations for the definition of the structuralistic method. There were two teachers, a native speaker and one speaking the same language as the students, who also dealt with grammar teaching.

Aural-oral approach or Audiolingual method

It is a method of foreign language teaching where the emphasis is on learning grammatical and phonological structure, especially for speaking and listening. It is based on behaviourism and so relies on formation as a basis for learning, through a great deal of mechanical repetition.

Authentic material

It describes the didactic use of materials that were originally for non-didactic purposes: newspaper articles, train tickets, films, advertisements, etc.

Blended learning

It is a didactic planning strategy that combines aspects and methods of traditional learning with aspects and methods of online learning. A course can be defined as blended learning where, alongside seminars, traditional lessons or training experiences carried out in the workplace, there are also moments of learning via CD-ROM, Web-based training, use of videos, etc. Blended learning training is a solution that is achieving success both in effectiveness and in popularity. Thanks to its flexibility and the centrality of the interpersonal communication dimension, technology allows a new type of learning that leverages processes as well as contents. This is the so-called Learning 2.0 that puts together the constructivist approach with multimedia learning. Here are some examples of a blended approach that can be easily created or used by teachers:

• eBook (achievable, for example, with the Scriptaweb software): manages to transform the online experience from a simple remote replication of interactions;

• educational blog (for example Blogger, Wordpress, Tumblr) has a more informal role in the identity negotiation and communication processes between students and with the teacher and acts as a real bridge between the classroom and the network, in the perfect blended spirit;

• online platforms. They can be a support for the main study and processing activity requested on the blog and eBook.

Blending see Word formation

Bottom-up vs Top-down
Bottom-up processing happens when someone tries to understand language by looking at individual meanings or grammatical characteristics of the most basic units of the text, (e.g. sounds for listening or words for reading) and moves from these to try to understand the whole text. Bottom-up processing is not thought to be a very efficient way to approach a text initially and is often contrasted with top-down processing, which is thought to be more efficient. Top-down processing of language happens when someone uses background information to predict the meaning of the language they are going to listen to or read. Rather than relying first on the actual words or sounds (bottom-up), they develop expectations about what they will hear or read, and confirm or reject these as they listen or read. Top-down processing is thought to be an effective way of processing language; it makes the most of what the person brings to the situation.

Brainstorming
Brainstorming is one of the techniques for identifying ideas, albeit in an unorganized way. It is a form of anticipation.

Cataphora see Anaphora

CBT
Computer-based testing, or CBT, is testing using a computer for all or part of the test. Computer-based testing is cheaper, more accessible and easier to administer than manual forms of testing but there are limitations, as CBT which evaluates speaking or writing still requires human examiners.

Chunks
They are groups of words that can be found together in language. They can be words that always go together, such as fixed collocations, or that commonly do, such as certain grammatical structures that follow rules. A listener or reader uses their knowledge of chunks to help them predict meaning and therefore be

able to process language in real time. Chunks include lexical phrases, set phrases, and fixed phrases.

Class round-up

It is an activity where the teacher and learners summarise what they have been doing during the class. Class round-ups are important not only to focus learners' attention on information but also to help the process of remembering it.

Cloze

It consists of inserting the missing words into a text. Usually, the first lines of the text are left intact to allow a first contextualization, then every seventh word is eliminated. It is used to develop and measure the ability to consider a text in its entirety, grasping any contextual and co-textual redundancy for understanding.

Class-centred teaching

It draws attention to the importance of behaving in ways that encourage classes to develop into cohesive groups in which learning is regarded as a collective, collaborative endeavour and the performance of individuals is lifted by the positive atmosphere of the overall class group.

Clause

It is a phrase that contains a verb and normally a subject. It can be a full sentence by itself or be part of a sentence. A <u>noun clause</u> is a clause that is used in the same way as a noun or a pronoun. A <u>relative clause</u> is a clause that tells us more about a noun or a noun phrase. There are two types, defining and non-defining. Defining add essential information to tell us what we are talking about, non-defining add extra information. A <u>subordinate - or dependent - clause</u> is a clause that adds more information to a sentence but is incomplete and not a sentence on its own. It functions like a noun, adverb or adjective. An <u>adverbial clause</u> tells us more about the main clause, in the same way as an adverb tells us more about a verb.

Cleft sentence

It is made by separating a single clause into two clauses, one main and one subordinate. Cleft sentences are useful to change emphasis; for example, compare 'You stole the money' and 'It was you who stole the money, not him'.

CLIL

Content and Language Integrated Learning, or CLIL, is where a subject is taught in the target language rather than the first language of the learners. In CLIL classes, tasks are designed to allow students to focus on and learn to use the new language as they learn the new subject content.

Clipping see Word formation

Coherence

It defines the logical, semantic network of the text and refers to the "rhetorical" aspects of your writing, which include developing and supporting your argument.

Cohesion

Cohesion is the network of internal formal references to a text and refers to the connection of your ideas both at the sentence level and at the paragraph level.

Cognate see False friend

Cognitive-code approach

Popular in the 1970s, it emphasised that language learning involved active mental processes, that it was not just a process of habit formation (the assumption underlying the audiolingual method that came before it). Lessons focussed on learning grammatical structures but the cognitive code approach emphasised the importance of meaningful practice, and the structures were presented inductively, i.e. the rules came after exposure to examples. There was, however, little use of examples from authentic material.

Cognitive strategies

Cognitive strategies are one type of learning strategy that learners use to learn more successfully. These include repetition, organising new language, summarising meaning, guessing meaning from context, using imagery for memorisation. All of these strategies involve deliberate manipulation of language to improve learn-learning. Classifications of learning strategies distinguish between cognitive strategies and two other types, metacognitive strategies (organising learning), and social/ affective strategies (which enable interaction).

Collocation

It refers to words that are found together in language. Collocations can be fixed, where it is difficult to replace one of the words with an alternative, or freer, allowing for more choice of words. 'Make a noise' or 'bright imagination'.

Competence vs Performance[12]

Competence is said to be an idealised conception of language, which is seen in opposition to the notion of performance which refers to the specific utterances of speech. Competence involves "knowing" the language and performance involves "doing" something with the language.

Communicative approach

It is the best-known current approach to language teaching. Task-based teaching is a methodology associated with it.

Communicative competence[13]

Communicative competence refers to a learner's ability to use the language correctly to communicate appropriately and effectively in a variety of social situations. It is constructed of four competency areas: linguistic, sociolinguistic, discourse, and strategic. Two of them focus on the functional aspect of communication, and the other two reflect the use of the linguistic system.

Connotation and Denotation

---

[12] Chomsky, Noam, *Aspects of the Theory of Syntax*, MIT Press, 1965

[13] Canale, M. and Swain, M. *Approaches to Communicative Competence. Singapore*: SEAMEO Regional Centre, 1980

Connotation refers to the wide array of positive and negative associations that most words naturally carry with them, whereas denotation is the precise, literal definition of a word that might be found in a dictionary.

Consonant cluster

A consonant cluster in a word is a group of consonants with no vowels between them. The longest possible cluster in English is three consonant sounds at the start, such as 'splash', and four at the end, as in 'twelfths'. The tongue twister 'The sixth twisty crisp' has several consonant clusters in it, making it difficult to pronounce.

Content words vs Grammatical words

Content words are words that have meaning. They can be compared to grammatical words, which are structural. Nouns, main verbs, adjectives, and adverbs are usually content words. Auxiliary verbs, pronouns, articles, and prepositions are usually grammatical words. It is an important difference in pronunciation between content and grammatical words. Content words tend to be stressed and grammatical words are often pronounced in a reduced form or with a schwa sound.

Contextualisation

It consists of putting language items into a meaningful and real context rather than being treated as isolated items of language for language manipulation practice only. Contextualising language tries to give real communicative value to the language that learners meet.

Cooperative learning

It "is a successful teaching strategy in which small teams, each with students of different levels of ability, use a variety of learning activities to improve their understanding of a subject. Each member of a team is responsible not only for learning what is taught but also for helping team-mates learn, thus creating an atmosphere of achievement. improves academic achievement strengthens communication skills.

Criterion-referenced tests vs Norm-referenced test

A criterion-referenced test measures a candidate's mark against a series of criteria and produces a description of level based on that criterion. It can be compared with a norm-referenced test, which places a learner's mark against what other people are achieving in the same test. Criterion-based tests are useful for indicating how a group of learners is progressing as they compare candidates against a standard, rather than each other. E.g.: IELTS and TOEFL are criterion-based tests. A norm-referenced test measures a candidate's mark against what other people are achieving in the same test. It can be compared with a criterion-referenced test, which measures a candidate's mark against a series of criteria and produces a description of level based on those criteria. Norm-based tests are useful for indicating the level of an individual learner in comparison with others. E.g.: SAT (Standardized Admission Test) in the United States.

(The) Critical Period Hypothesis

There is a period of growth in which full native competence is possible when acquiring a language. This period is from early childhood to adolescence. The critical period hypothesis has implications for teachers and learning programmes, but it is not universally accepted. Acquisition theories say that adults do not acquire languages as well as children because of external and internal factors, not because of a lack of ability.

Curriculum

It refers to the lessons and academic content taught in a school or a specific course or program.

De-lexicalised verbs

They are verbs that have little meaning alone but that can be joined together with many other words, so generating a wide variety of new meanings. These have also been called 'empty' verbs. 'Get' is a common example of this. 'Get' does not have one single meaning but can be linked with many other words to generate meanings, e.g. *get in, get away, get married, get paid, get older, get more difficult*, etc.

Deductive Approach see Inductive approach

Diagnostic test see Achievement test

Diphthong
It is a one-syllable sound that is made up of two vowels. In Received Pronunciation English there are eight diphthong sounds. The sound /ei/ in play and made is a diphthong made up of two vowel sounds, /e/ and /i/.

Direct Method
It was developed as a response to the Grammar-Translation method. It sought to immerse the learner in the same way as when a first language is learnt. All teaching is done in the target language, grammar is taught inductively, there is a focus on speaking and listening, and only useful 'everyday' language is taught. The weakness in the Direct Method is its assumption that a second language can be learnt in the same way as a first, when in fact the conditions under which a second language is learnt are very different.

Discourse management
It refers to the ability to produce extended written and spoken texts, for example, conversations. It is often a criterion in formal evaluation of spoken and written language.

Drill
It is a classroom technique used to practise new language. It involves the teacher modelling a word or a sentence and the learners repeating it. E.g.: Teacher: I like cheese > Learners: I like it > Teacher: I like apples > Learners: I like them > Teacher: I like Sue etc.

EAP/ESP
EAP or English for Academic Purposes refers to learning English to use it to study another subject. ESP or English for Specific Purposes refers to learning English because you have a specific need. It can include the area of EPP, English for Professional Purposes.

(The) Eclectic approach

It is the label given to a teacher's use of techniques and activities from a range of language teaching approaches and methodologies. The teacher decides what methodology or approach to use depending on the aims of the lesson and the learners in the group. Almost all modern coursebooks have a mixture of approaches and methodologies.

EFL/ESL

EFL or English as a Foreign Language refers to learning and using English as an additional language in a non-English speaking country. ESL or English as a Second Language refers mainly to learning English as a new resident in an English-speaking country.

Ellipsis

It is the omission of one or more words from a sentence, where they are unnecessary because they have already been mentioned. 'As it has the last three ( )' = a noun phrase is omitted; 'Yes, I have ( )'. = verbal ellipsis.

Elicitation

Techniques or procedures which a teacher uses to get learners to actively produce speech or writing. It helps to develop a learner-centred classroom and a stimulating environment and makes making learning memorable by linking new and old information.

Embedding

It refers to the process of inserting one sentence into another sentence. It includes putting questions into affirmative sentences, with a subsequent change in word order (embedded questions). E.g.: 'I wonder if you could tell me what time it is?' is the question 'What time is it?' embedded in a polite structure.

Englishes see Lingua Franca

Error

In a communicative approach, errors represent a precious source of information to be analysed and corrected only when it prevents communication. When performing linguistic tasks what matters is its pragmatic efficacy, not its mere correctness.

False friends
They are words that look or sound the same as words in the learner's first language but are not so, causing the learner to make a mistake. They can be compared with cognates, which are words that are the same in different languages.

Feedback
It is information a teacher or another speaker, including another learner, gives to learners on how well they are doing, either to help the learner improve specific points, or to help plan their learning.

Flipped classroom
It is a form of blended learning that overturns the traditional learning system made up of frontal lessons, individual study at home and classroom questions, with a rather rigid and hierarchical student-teacher relationship. How does a flipped classroom work? The teacher, before tackling a topic in the classroom, assigns to his students some videos to watch at home. The students thus acquire the basic notions of the content to be treated, being able to devote the time available at school to clarifications, exercises and any other functional activity to better understand. Flipping does not simply mean delivering videos and worksheets, it requires a complete change in the way of planning. The teacher must have a clear understanding of the final objectives and desired outcomes to choose the most appropriate methodologies and resources for the educational success of the students. The role of the teacher is radically changed. No longer as a transmitter of culture - and the web is suitable for this purpose in a much more complete, versatile, updated, simple and economic way -, but a guide for the student in active processing and the development of complex tasks. On the basis of the success of each inverted class is the principle of sharing and collaboration between teachers and teachers between pupils and teachers, between pupils and pupils.

Fluency see Accuracy

Fossilization

It refers to the process in which incorrect language becomes a habit and cannot easily be corrected.

Function

The general social uses of language. In 1960, Jakobson[14] argued that the dominance of any one of six factors within an utterance reflects a different linguistic function: referential, expressive: conative, poetic (or aesthetic), phatic, and metalingual. In any given situation one of these factors is 'dominant', and this dominant function influences the general character of the message. In Halliday's linguistic typology[15], the seven basic functions identified in children's usage are heuristic, imaginative, informative, instrumental, interactional, personal, and regulative. He adds three adult metafunctions: ideational, interpersonal, and textual.

Gradable adjectives vs Non-gradable adjectives

Gradable adjectives are adjectives that have different degrees and so can be graded. They can be compared with non-gradable adjectives, which do not have degrees. Compare 'hot' > 'very hot' with 'red' > ~~'very red'~~.

Holistic approach

It sees language as a whole, which is not divisible in a meaningful way when teaching. This contrasts with an atomistic approach to language, which attempts to analyse language into parts, such as grammatical structures or functional exponents, which can later become the content of a syllabus. A holistic approach would focus on everything the learner needs to know to communicate effectively.

Homonym

---

[14] Jakobson, R., *Linguistics and Poetics*, in T. Sebeok, ed., Style in Language, Cambridge, MA: M.I.T. Press, 1960

[15] Halliday, M. A. K. (1985) *An Introduction to Functional Grammar*, London: Arnold

A word that has the same sound or spelling as another but a different meaning. Homonyms can be separated into two groups, homographs (same spelling) and homophones (same sound).

Homophone
It is a word that has the same sound as another word but different meaning and spelling. This can be compared with a homonym, which has the same spelling and sounds the same but has a different meaning.

Hyponyms
They are words that are the specific examples of a general word, a 'superordinate'. They can be compared with synonyms, which mean the same things, and antonyms, which mean opposite things. E.g.: red, white and blue are all colours.

ICT
ICT or Information and Communication Technology refers to technological tools that are used to communicate and to manage information. Interactive Whiteboards are an example of ICT.

Inductive approach vs Deductive Approach
An inductive approach starts with examples and asks learners to find rules. It can be compared with a deductive approach that starts by giving learners rules, then examples, then practice. A deductive approach to teaching language starts by giving learners rules, then examples, then practice. It is a teacher-centred approach to presenting new content.

Inference see Reference

Information gap task
It is a technique in language teaching where students are missing information necessary to complete a task or solve a problem and must communicate with their classmates to fill in the gaps. It is often used in communicative language teaching and task-based language learning. Information gap tasks are contrasted with opinion gap tasks, in which all information is shared at the start of the

activity, and learners give their own opinions on the information given.

Input
It refers to the exposure learners have to authentic language in use. This can be from various sources, including the teacher, other learners, and the environment around the learners. Input can be compared to intake, which is input then taken in and internalized by the learner so it can be applied.

(The) Input Hypothesis
One of the 5 hypotheses of Krashen's Theory of Second Language Acquisition. the learner improves and progresses along with the 'natural order' when he/she receives second language 'input' that is one step beyond his/her current stage of linguistic competence. For example, if a learner is at a stage 'i', then acquisition takes place when he/she is exposed to 'Comprehensible Input' that belongs to level 'i + 1'.

Interactional language see Transactional language

Intercultural communicative competence
It refers to the ability to understand cultures, including your own, and use this understanding to communicate with people from other cultures successfully.

Interlanguage
It is the learner's current version of the language they are learning. Interlanguage changes all the time but can become fossilised language when the learners do not have the opportunity to improve.

Intonation
It is the way the pitch of a speaker's voice goes up or down as they speak. Intonation can be rising, falling or flat and is used to communicate how a speaker feels.

Intransitive verbs see Transitive verbs

IPA
The International Phonetic Alphabet is an alphabetic system of phonetic notation based primarily on the Latin alphabet.

Jigsaw
It is a cooperative learning strategy that enables each student of a "home" group to specialize in one aspect of a topic (for example, one group studies habitats of rainforest animals, another group studies predators of rainforest animals). Students meet with members from other groups who are assigned the same aspect, and after mastering the material, return to the "home" group and teach the material to their group members. With this strategy, each student in the "home" group serves as a piece of the topic's puzzle and when they work together as a whole, they create the complete jigsaw puzzle.

Jumble
In a jumble activity, learners need to put sentences or paragraphs from a text, or pictures illustrating a text, into the correct order.

L1, L2, L3… & FL
L1 is the language that an individual has learnt since childhood. L2 is the language learnt in the country in which it is usually spoken, e.g. English in the UK. FL is a language generally studied at school, in a country where it is not usually spoken, e.g. English in Italian schools.

LAD
Language Acquisition Device. For Chomsky[16] it is a hypothetical tool hardwired into the brain that helps children rapidly learn and understand language It is used to explain how children can acquire language abilities as well as accounting for the innate understanding of grammar and syntax all children possess.

Language usage vs Language use

---

[16] Chomsky, Noam, Aspects of the Theory of Syntax, MIT Press, 1965

Language usage refers to the rules for making language, i.e. the structures used. It can be compared to use, which considers the communicative meaning of language.

Learning see Acquisition

Learners (types of)
In the field-dependent/independent model of cognitive or learning style, a field-dependent learning style is defined by a relative inability to distinguish detail from other information around it. Field-dependent learners often work well in teams as they tend to be better at interpersonal relationships. A field-independent learning style is defined by a tendency to separate details from the surrounding context. Field-independent learners tend to rely less on the teacher or other learners for support Theorists define these two cognitive styles in terms of how they are psychologically different - which makes this a useful model for teachers trying to understand their learners.

Lexical approach
It is a way of analysing and teaching language based on the idea that it is made up of lexical units rather than grammatical structures. The units are words, chunks formed by collocations, and fixed phrases.

Lexicon
It is often used to describe the knowledge that a speaker has about the words of a language. This includes meanings, use, form, and relationships with other words. A lexicon can thus be thought of as a mental dictionary.

Lingua franca and *Englishes*
Lingua franca is a language that is used widely outside the country where it is spoken as a native language. The current lingua franca of international business is English. The term *Englishes* refers to the many kinds of *Englishes* spoken around the world, both as a first and second language. One view holds that these are equally correct and valid. This lessens the importance of a 'standard' Eng-

lish, and questions giving priority to 'British' or 'American' English as targets for teaching English.

Loan words see Word formation

Meta-language

It is the language teachers and learners use to talk about the English language, learning, and teaching. Words and phrases such as 'verb', 'noun', 'present perfect continuous', 'phrasal verb' and 'reported speech' are all examples of common classroom meta-language.

Metacognitive awareness

It means being aware of how you think. In the ELT classroom, it means being aware of how you learn. Developing metacognitive awareness is an important part of helping learners become more effective and, importantly, more autonomous. If learners are conscious of how they learn then they can identify the most effective ways of doing so.

Mind maps

They are visual records of new vocabulary or other content. Vocabulary mind maps are also known as word maps or spidergrams and are organised in a way that shows groupings or relationships between the words.

Minimal pairs

They are pairs of words that only have one sound different. 'But' and 'bat' is a minimal pair. Only the vowel sound is different.

(The) Monitor Hypothesis[17]

One of the 5 hypotheses of Krashen's Theory of Second Language Acquisition. The monitoring function is the practical result of the learned grammar. According to Krashen, the acquisition system is the utterance initiator, while the learning system performs the role

---

[17] Krashen, Stephen D. *Principles and Practice in Second Language Acquisition*, Prentice-Hall International, 1987 and Krashen, Stephen D. *Second Language Acquisition and Second Language Learning*. Prentice-Hall International, 1988.

of the 'monitor' or the 'editor'. The 'monitor' acts in a planning, editing and correcting function.

Morpheme see Allomorph

Motivation
Intrinsic motivation is a motivation to learn that comes from an internal force such as interest in language learning or the desire for further personal development in general. It compares with extrinsic motivation, which is motivation from external pressures such as the need to speak English for work or because a parent has sent a learner to class.

Multiple intelligence theory
There are at least eight different kinds of intelligence, and that human beings possess all of them to different degrees. Learners' profiles of intelligence will affect their preferences when learning. Musical intelligence: when learners are more sensitive to music and often have clear musical ability; naturalistic intelligence: when learners are more sensitive to nature and to their role in nature; visual/spatial intelligence: when learners have a strong visual memory and are artistic; bodily/kinaesthetic intelligence: when learners may enjoy doing things rather than reading or hearing about them and are good at making things and at physical activities in general; logical/mathematical intelligence: when learners are often good at logical reasoning and scientific investigation; verbal-linguistic intelligence: when learners are good at languages and enjoy reading and writing; intrapersonal intelligence: when learners are introspective, prefer working alone, and are very self-aware; linguistic intelligence: when are good at languages and enjoy reading and writing.

(The) Natural Order Hypothesis[18]
One of the 5 hypotheses of Krashen's Theory of Second Language Acquisition. The acquisition of grammatical structures

---

[18] Krashen, Stephen D. *Principles and Practice in Second Language Acquisition.* Prentice-Hall International, 1987 and Krashen, Stephen D. *Second Language Acquisition and Second Language Learning.* Prentice-Hall International, 1988.

follows a 'natural order' which is predictable. For a given language, some grammatical structures tend to be acquired early while others late.

Neuro-linguistic Programming
It is based on a model of communication and psychotherapy. In ELT this model has implications for learning, as it says that we all have different learning and perceptual preferences, and to learn well we need to both exploit our preferred styles and develop our less preferred ones.

Norm-referenced test see Criterion-referenced tests

Objective tests vs Subjective tests
An objective test is a test that has right or wrong answers and so can be marked objectively. It can be compared with a subjective test, which is evaluated by giving an opinion, usually based on agreed criteria. Objective tests are popular because they are easy to prepare and take, quick to mark and provide a quantifiable and concrete result.

Observation checklist
It is a list of things that an observer is going to look at when observing a class. This list may have been prepared by the observer or the teacher or both. Observation checklists not only give an observer a structure and framework for an observation but also serve as a contract of understanding with the teacher, who may, as a result, be more comfortable, and will get specific feedback on aspects of the class. Questions that may be included are:
- Does the teacher follow the timings on the lesson plan?
- Does the teacher tell learners how long they have for an activity?
- Does the teacher tell learners when time is nearly up?

Pair work
It is learners working together in pairs. One of the main motivations to encourage pair work in the English language classroom is to increase the opportunities for learners to use English in the class.

Peer correction
It is a classroom technique where learners correct each other, rather than the teacher doing this.

Performance see Competence

Phonemes vs Allophones
They are the smallest units of sounds in a language. If a phoneme is changed, the word may change, e.g. change the l sound in 'lack' to a b and the word changes to 'back'. Allomorphs are different forms of the same morpheme or basic unit of meaning. These can be different pronunciations or different spellings. There are three allomorphs of the morpheme -s in English. Compare the sound of the -s in 'cats', 'dogs' and 'foxes'.

Phonetics vs phonology
Phonetics is the study of human speech. Phonetics includes the study of how sounds are physically produced (by positioning the mouth, lips, and tongue), and how sounds are perceived by a listener. Phonetics can be compared to phonology, which is the study of the particular sound units (phonemes) of language.

Phonics
It is a method of teaching young learners how to read which focuses on how letters make sounds, and how these sounds make words. It can be compared with the whole word, or 'Look and say' approach, which focuses on recognising words.

Phonology see Phonetics

Polysemy
It refers to the quality of some words to have several related meanings. A word which has several related meanings is thus a polyseme. These can be compared to homonyms, which are words that have several completely different meanings. E.g.: head

Portfolios

The Council of Europe uses Language Portfolios as part of its framework for the learning of European languages. It is a collection of work prepared, maintained and developed by a learner. Portfolios can contain information about the learner and their learning experiences, and examples of their work.

PPP
It stands for presentation, production, and practice. And represents a model used to describe typical stages of a presentation of new language. The practice stage aims to provide opportunities for learners to use the target structure. Criticism of this paradigm argues that the freer 'practice' stage may not elicit the target language as it is designed to do, as, in this meaning-based stage, students communicate with any language they can. It is not clear that forcing students to use certain structures to communicate in a practice activity will necessarily mean they will use these structures spontaneously later. PPP tends to be teacher-centred, as the teacher leads the activity and provides the necessary information, usually in an open-class arrangement.

Prefixes see Affixes

Productive skills see Ability

Proficiency see Achievement tests

Prosodic features
They are features that appear when we put sounds together in connected speech. It is as important to teach learners prosodic features as successful communication depends as much on intonation, stress, and rhythm as on the correct pronunciation of sounds. Intonation, stress, and rhythm are prosodic features.

Receptive skills see Ability

RP
RP or received pronunciation refers to an accent in English regarded by many people as a 'standard' accent. It has also been called 'the Queen's English' or 'BBC English'. In the past, RP had high

status in the UK, indicating an educated speaker, and this transferred into EFL where it has been used as a model for pronunciation. With the emergence of international English, the recognition of the equality of a variety of accents, and the emphasis on authentic communication, learners now become aware of a wider range of accents.

Reading techniques

<u>Extensive reading</u> involves learners reading texts for enjoyment and to develop general reading skills. <u>Intensive reading</u> means reading in detail with specific learning aims and tasks. <u>Skimming</u> corresponds to reading a text for gist, i.e. the general meaning or purpose of a text. <u>Scanning</u> is reading a text quickly to find specific information, e.g. figures or names.

Register

It often refers to the degree of formality of language, but in a more general sense, it means the language used by a group of people who share similar work or interests, such as doctors or lawyers. Compare 'Would you mind passing the salt?' with 'Pass me the salt'.

Reference vs Inference

Reference is the use of a linguistic form to enable a listener/reader to identify something. Inference denotes the process of decoding the pragmatic meaning of an utterance. To do so, the listener uses additional knowledge to make sense of what has not been explicitly said.

Reliability see Validity

Rubric

It refers to the written instructions for a task.

Schwa

It is an unstressed vowel sound which occurs in many words of two syllables or more and in connected speech. It is the most common vowel sound in English and is represented by the symbol below.

Semantics
It is the study of how meaning is created by words. It is sometimes compared with syntax, which concerns the rules that dictate how sentences are formed.

(The) Silent Period Hypothesis
It is the idea that when a language is learned, there should be a period in which the learner is not expected to actively produce any language. This is based on observations of a listening period in infants when they learn a first language.

Silent way
It is a methodology of teaching language based on the idea that teachers should be as silent as possible during a class but learners should be encouraged to speak as much as possible.

Skill see Ability

Sociocultural awareness
It means awareness of the societies and cultures of the target language, and therefore of the contexts, the language is used in. Teachers themselves transmit information subconsciously about culture and society through their behaviour and interaction with learners.

Stative verbs
They are verbs that describe a state. They can be compared with action or dynamic verbs, which describe an action. Know, love, have are stative verbs.

Stress
It is the emphasis given to certain syllables in words. In English, stress is produced with a longer, louder and higher-pitched sound than unstressed sounds.

Stress-timed languages see Syllable-timed languages

Suffixes see Affixes

STT vs TTT
STT means Student Talking Time. It is the time learners spend talking rather than the teacher. It can be compared with Teacher Talking Time (TTT). It can be a useful category for the observation of teaching, or self-reflection about teaching.

Subjective tests see Objective tests

Syllable-timed languages vs Stress-timed languages
A syllable-timed language is a language whose syllables take approximately equal amounts of time to pronounce. It can be compared with a stress-timed language, where there is approximately the same amount of time between stressed syllables. Learners whose first language can be described as syllable-timed often have problems recognising and then producing features of English such as contractions, main and secondary stress, and elision. French is described as a syllable-timed language, English as a stress-timed one

Syllabus
It is a document that describes what the contents of a language course will be and the order in which they will be taught. The content of a syllabus normally reflects certain beliefs about language and language learning. A process-oriented syllabus focuses on the skills and processes involved in learning language. It can be compared with a product-oriented syllabus, which focuses on completed acts of communication, the outputs. A task-based syllabus is based on task-based learning, an approach where learners carry out tasks such as solving a problem or planning an activity. A grammatical syllabus is based on the structures of a language. It can be compared to other types of syllabi based around tasks, vocabulary, functions or topics. Learners learn grammatical structures in a sequence that reflects their complexity, rather than their use in communication, leading to many artificial contexts for practice, and perhaps an inability to transfer learning to real communication. Organising learning around a grammatical syllabus has been criticised because of this, but it is still the most common type of syllabus in published

materials, mostly because it is the easiest type of syllabus to sequence.

Syntax
It is the study of the rules that control how language is structured first into clauses and then sentences. It can be compared with semantics, which is the study of how meaning is created by words.

Taboo language
In language learning, taboo language or subjects are areas that are regarded as prohibited by the culture of the learners or the teacher, therefore inappropriate for the classroom.

Tag questions
They are short questions that speakers use at the end of a statement. If the intonation of the tag is falling, then the speaker is asking for confirmation of the statement. If it is rising, then the speaker is unsure and is, in fact, asking a question. There are rules for the formation of tag questions.

Target language
It is the language learners are studying, and also the individual items of language that they want to learn, or the teacher wants them to learn. In a PPP lesson, the teacher first presents the target language, learners practise it, and then there is a production stage where the target language is used in a freer activity.

Top-down see Bottom-up

TPR
TPR means Total Physical Response. It is an approach to teaching language based on the idea that if you have to do something physical in response to language, then learning is more meaningful, and you learn faster.

Transactional language vs interactional language
Transactional language is language that is used to make a transaction and which has a result. It can be compared with interactional language, which is used to maintain relationships.

Transitive verbs vs Intransitive verbs
Transitive verbs have an object. They can be contrasted with <u>intransitive verbs</u>, which do not need an object.

TTT see STT

Unvoiced consonants vs Voiced consonants
Unvoiced consonants are consonant sounds that are made without vibrating the vocal chords: /p/ as in 'pet' /t/ as in 'top' /k/ as in 'cat'. Voiced consonants are consonant sounds that are made by vibrating the vocal chords: /b/ as in 'bed' /d/ as in 'dip' /g/ as in 'good' /ð/ as in 'the'.

Validity and Reliability (tests)
A test's validity refers to how good it is. Validity can be compared with reliability, which refers to how consistent the results would be if the test were given under the same conditions to the same learners.

VAK
VAK, or Visual, Auditory and Kinesthetic, refers to one model of learning styles. The VAK model is comprised of three different learning styles or preferred ways of learning. In some accounts, another style, tactile, is included.

Voiced consonant see Unvoiced consonant

Weak forms
They are syllable sounds that become unstressed in connected speech and are often then pronounced as a schwa.

Webquest
It is an activity that requires learners to use the Internet to complete a task. Webquests can extend over an entire course, several classes or be integrated into a single lesson.

Word formation

It refers to the creation of new words. <u>Blending</u> refers to joining the beginning of one word and the end of another to make a new word with a new meaning. (smoke + fog = smog). <u>Clipping</u> involves the shortening of a longer word, often reducing it to one syllable. Many examples are very informal or slang. Maths > mathematics, or 'bro' > brother (informal). <u>Loan words</u> from other languages (parasol), and <u>acronyms</u> (scuba) are other examples of ways new words are formed.

Word stress

It indicates which syllables are stressed - or emphasised - in a word. 'Photograph' has word stress Ooo (stress on the first syllable), 'photographer' has word stress oOoo (stress on the second syllable).

References

- Gower R., Phillips D., Walters S., Teaching Practice Handbook, Heinemann, Oxford 1995
- Northern College, Writing a Lesson Plan
- Ellis G. & Sinclair B., (1989) Learning to Learn English, Cambridge University Press
- http://www.slideshare.net/yseauy/lesson-plan-powerpoint-presentation
- http://jfmueller.faculty.noctrl.edu/205/madelinehunter.htmhh
- http://www.youtubeh.com/watch?v=y3WT07eFHX0&feature=youtube_gdata_playero
- DPR 89/2010 e DM ;
- DPR 88/2010;
- DPR 87/2010
- Circolare Ministeriale 8/2013;
- Direttiva del 27/12/2012;
- Richards, Jack C.; Schmidt, Richard, eds. (2009). "Information gap". Longman Dictionary of Language Teaching and Applied Linguistics. New York: Longman. p. 282.
- Ellis, Rod (2003). Task-Based Language Learning and Teaching. Oxford: Oxford University Press
- Larsen-Freeman, Diane (2000). Techniques and Principles in Language Teaching. Oxford: Oxford University Press.
- Common European Framework of Reference for Languages: Learning, teaching, assessment (CEFR), EU, 2001
- http://www.slideshare.net/yseauy/lesson-plan-powerpoint-presentation
- http://jfmueller.faculty.noctrl.edu/205/madelinehunter.htmhh
- www.brighthubeducation.com/special-ed-inclusion-strategies
- http://www.youtubeh.com/watch?v=y3WT07eFHX0&feature=youtube_gdata_playero
- http://nuovilicei.indire.it/content/index.php?action=lettura&id_m=7782&id_cnt=10497
- Heidi Jacobs, Interdisciplinary Curriculum: Design and Implementation, Alexandria, VA: Association for Supervision and Curriculum Design, (1989), p. 8
- http://www.educ.ualberta.ca/staff/olenka.bilash/best%20of%20bilash/info%20gap%20activities.html
- Willis, J. (1996), A Framework for Task-Based Learning. Longman
- Dodman, M., course of Metodologia della lingua Inglese e nuove tecnologie, SILSIS – Pavia, a.a. 2002/03- 2003/04
- Ranzoli, S., course of Metodologia dell'insegnamento del testo letterario inglese, SILSIS – Pavia, a.a. 2002/03
- Ellis, D. J., Literature for life, 2011, Loescher Editore
- Spiazzi, Tavella, Layton, *Performer Culture & Literature 1*, Bologna, 2012
- www.answersingenesis.org/articles/cm/v12/n3/sir-isaac-newton
- https://www.britannica.com/biography/John-Milton
- Widdowson, H. G. (1998) *Teaching Language as Communication*. OUP. Oxford.
- Krashen, Stephen D. *Principles and Practice in Second Language Acquisition.* Prentice-Hall International, 1987.
- Krashen, Stephen D. *Second Language Acquisition and Second Language Learning.* Prentice-Hall International, 1988.
- Chomsky, Noam, *Aspects of the Theory of Syntax*, MIT Press, 1965

- Canale, M. and Swain, M. *Approaches to Communicative Competence*. Singapore: SEAMEO Regional Centre, 1980
- https://www.edglossary.org/
- https://www.teachingenglish.org.uk/
- Halliday, M. A. K. (1985) *An Introduction to Functional Grammar*, London: Arnold
- Jakobson, R., Linguistics and Poetics, in T. Sebeok, ed., Style in Language, Cambridge, MA: M.I.T. Press, 1960
- https://www.mindomo.com/it/dashboard

Images
- www.freeworldmaps.net
- https://commons.wikimedia.org/wiki/File:Blitzaftermath.jpg
- https://commons.wikimedia.org/wiki/File:Blitz_West_End_Air_Shelter.jpg
- https://commons.wikimedia.org/wiki/File:A_pilot_of_No._175_Squadron_RAF_scrambles_to_his_waiting_Hawker_Typhoon_Mk_IB_fighter-bomber_at_Le_Fresne-Camilly_in_Normandy,_24_July_1944._CL570.jpg
- https://commons.wikimedia.org/wiki/File:Hitler_Will_Send_No_Warning_Art.IWMPST13861.jpg
- https://en.wikipedia.org/wiki/File:World_War_I,_British_soccer_team_with_gas_masks,_1916.jpg
- https://commons.wikimedia.org/wiki/File:WWII_Food_Rationing.jpg
- https://commons.wikimedia.org/wiki/File:INF3-164_Britain_expects_that_you_too,_this_day,_will_do_your_duty_Artist_Forster.jpg
- https://en.wikipedia.org/wiki/British_propaganda_during_World_War_II
- https://commons.wikimedia.org/wiki/File:Sir_Winston_Churchill_-_19086236948.jpg
- https://it.m.wikipedia.org/wiki/File:The_Yalta_Conference,_February_1945_NAM234.jpg
- https://en.wikipedia.org/wiki/File:William_Blake_Hamlet_and_his_Father%27s_Ghost_1806_British_Museum.jpg
- https://commons.wikimedia.org/wiki/File:Eug%C3%A8ne_Delacroix_Hamlet_und_Horatio_auf_dem_Friedhof_(1835)_St%C3%A4del_Museum.jpg
- https://commons.wikimedia.org/wiki/File:The_Execution_of_Charles_I_of_England.jpg
- https://it.wikipedia.org/wiki/File:Charles_I_(1630s).jpg
- https://www.flickr.com/photos/60861613@N00/3922655585
- https://it.wikipedia.org/wiki/Puritani#/media/File:John_Pettie_Puritan_Roundhead.jpg
- https://en.wikipedia.org/wiki/Force#/media/File:GodfreyKneller-IsaacNewton-1689.jpg
- https://commons.wikimedia.org/wiki/File:ParadiseLLinell3.jpg
- https://it.m.wikipedia.org/wiki/File:Blake,_William_(English,_1757%E2%80%931827),_%27Satan_Watching_the_Caresses_of_Adam_and_Eve%27_(Illustration_to_%27Paradise_Lost%27),_1808,_pen;_watercolor_on_paper,_50.5_x_38_cm,_Museum_of_Fine_Arts,_Boston,_US.jpg
- https://commons.wikimedia.org/wiki/File:St_Pauls_aerial_(cropped).jpg
- https://commons.wikimedia.org/wiki/File:Great_Gate,_Hampton_Court_Palace.jpg
- https://it.m.wikipedia.org/wiki/File:Naval_College.JPG
- https://rm.wikipedia.org/wiki/Datoteca:Colosseo.JPG
- https://it.wikipedia.org/wiki/File:Firenze_Palazzo_della_Signoria,_better_known_as_the_Palazzo_Vecchio.jpg
- https://commons.wikimedia.org/wiki/File:Milan_Cathedral_from_Piazza_del_Duomo.jpg
- https://it.wikipedia.org/wiki/File:Venezia_-_Panorama_007,_San_Marco_e_Palazzo_ducale.jpg
- https://www.flickr.com/photos/eager/11833679286

- https://commons.wikimedia.org/wiki/File:British_Indian_Empire_1909_Imperial_Gazetteer_of_India.jpg
- https://pixabay.com/it/photos/mohandas-karamchand-gandhi-67483/
- https://commons.wikimedia.org/wiki/File:Gandhi_costume.jpg
- https://commons.wikimedia.org/wiki/File:British_Indian_Empire_1909_Imperial_Gazetteer_of_India.jpg
- https://commons.wikimedia.org/wiki/File:Mahatma_Gandhi%27s_funeral_procession.jpg
- https://www.flickr.com/photos/joezach/218660271
- https://en.wikipedia.org/wiki/Indira_Gandhi#/media/File:Gandhi_and_Indira_1924.jpg
- https://commons.wikimedia.org/wiki/File:Bombay_Chronicle_January_26_1931.jpg
- https://commons.wikimedia.org/wiki/File:Gandhi_outside_10_Downing_Street,_London.jpg
- https://commons.wikimedia.org/wiki/File:Mahatma_Gandhi_with_women_textile_workers_at_Darwen,_Lancashire.jpg
- https://it.wikipedia.org/wiki/File:Flag_of_India.svg

Printed by Amazon Italia Logistica S.r.l.
Torrazza Piemonte (TO), Italy